How Our Ancestors Lived

JEWISH LIVES

Britain 1750–1950

A Guide for Family Historians

Melody Amsel-Arieli

Pen & Sword
FAMILY HISTORY

First published in Great Britain in 2013 by
PEN & SWORD FAMILY HISTORY
an imprint of
Pen & Sword Books Ltd
47 Church Street
Barnsley
South Yorkshire
S70 2AS

ISBN 978 1 84884 411 7

A CIP catalogue record for this book is
available from the British Library.

Typeset in Palatino and Optima by
CHIC GRAPHICS

Printed and bound in England by
MPG Printgroup, UK

Pen & Sword Books Ltd incorporates the imprints of
Pen & Sword Aviation, Pen & Sword Maritime, Pen & Sword Military,
Wharncliffe Local History, Pen & Sword Select, Pen & Sword
Military Classics, Leo Cooper, The Praetorian Press, Remember When,
Seaforth Publishing and Frontline Publishing

For a complete list of Pen & Sword titles please contact
PEN & SWORD BOOKS LTD
47 Church Street, Barnsley, South Yorkshire, S70 2AS, England
E-mail: enquiries@pen-and-sword.co.uk
Website: www.pen-and-sword.co.uk

CONTENTS

In Memory,
Sally Anita Amsel

ACKNOWLEDGEMENTS

I would like to thank the following for their contributions to this publication:

Contributors

Gary Nelson, da Costa descendant
Lois Kaufman, Myers and Ze'ev Yitzhak Dovid HaLevi/Davis descendant
Shimon Frais, Wolfsohn/Woolfson and Donn descendant
Alex Pelican and Paul Auerbach, Pelikan/Pelican descendants
Bryan Diamond and Judith Silver, Hauzer/Hauser descendants
Michael Glazer, Bederov/Bedeman and Glazer descendant
Alan Cohen, Glazer descendant
Judith Elam, Mendzigursky descendant
Alan Ehrlich, Wolfsohn/Woolfson family history researcher
Chris Hobbs, Sheffield family history researcher

Archives
Gillian Kirby, The National Archives of the United Kingdom
Miriam Rodrigues-Pereira, Honorary Archivist, Bevis Marks Spanish and Portuguese Jews' Congregation
The Rothschild Archive, London
Christine Wilde, The Greater Manchester Police Museum and Archives

Personal
Moira Feinsilver
Anne Jaron
Jeanette R. Rosenberg
and Nomi Dror, Etai Gross, and Mickey Arieli – always

Rupert Harding, Simon Fowler, Richard Doherty and their colleagues at Pen & Sword

INTRODUCTION

According to tradition, all Jewish souls, born and not yet born, were present when Moses received the Ten Commandments at Mount Sinai. All stood in God's presence as one, interconnected.

Since then, war, expulsions, persecution and immigration have dispersed untold numbers around the world. In recent years, many of their descendants, exploring their roots, have begun re-weaving the severed strands of Jewish history.

Jewish Lives presents the life-stories of ten Jews who, between 1750 and 1950, left Portugal, The Netherlands, Congress-Poland, Prussian-Poland, the Russian Empire, the Austro-Hungarian Empire and Nazi Germany for Great Britain.

Along with exploring their backgrounds and origins, these tales, arranged chronologically, also discuss the historical, social and economic forces that encouraged these immigrants to dream of distant shores. Since each tale is based on actual research shared by an amateur-genealogist descendant, methods and resources, whether cited in text or in supplemental document lists, vary.

Sources vary not only from chapter to chapter, but also by time and place. Early Dutch Jewish records, for example, are accessible online. Eastern European documentation, available through The Latter Day Saints Library as well as in scattered archives, generally begins with the nineteenth century mandatory adoption of Jewish surnames. Jewishgen.org, in cooperation with the Jewish Genealogical Society of Great Britain and other sources, offers a wealth of resources ranging from the mid-1700s through the present.

Early European travel documents – if they existed at all – evidently disappeared in natural disasters, fires, war, or times of political upheaval. Between 1850 and 1934, however, German authorities maintained records of passengers who departed the port of Hamburg.

British historical material, scarce through the 1700s, also becomes more plentiful as time goes by. Select travel documents, relating to aliens and naturalisations, exist from 1794, and relevant trade directories appear soon after. Certain synagogue vital records (some of which reveal earlier information through derivation) exist well before mandatory registration in 1837. British census records exist from 1841 on. Relevant newspaper and eye-witness accounts, insurance records, letters, and handwritten testimonials abound by the 1860s. Naturalisation records become more common after 1915, as do military records. Memorial volumes, which offer descriptions, histories, photographs, maps and memories of many destroyed Jewish communities, appear after the Holocaust.

These primary sources, naturally, are subject to error. Careless census enumerators or clerks sometimes suffered poor penmanship, or recorded incorrect or partial information. Subjects themselves, wishing to appear younger, older or to mislead authorities, sometimes falsified information. Moreover, researchers themselves sometimes err in translation, transliteration or interpretation. Moreover, spellings of names often vary.

My contributors, by sharing personal diaries, narratives, photographs, memories and family lore, also added invaluable depth to their ancestors' lives.

Although nearly all chapters officially feature men, their wives, though they may have left more modest paper trails, played equally significant roles. In addition to raising scores of children, running households and shaping family identities, they took in boarders, ran grocery shops, sold books, manned market stalls, peddled matches and stitched caps. Some even founded cinemas or inspired buildings.

Jewish Lives, seen as a whole, not only explores two hundred years of Jewish life from Portugal to Bessarabia, from the Inquisition through the Holocaust, but also traces the development of Anglo-Jewry.

Hopefully, these tales will inspire historians and researchers – Jewish and non-Jews alike – to explore their own family histories. Hopefully, they will discover meaningful parallels between their lives and the lives of those who came before them.

Melody Amsel-Arieli
North Branch, New Jersey to Beersheba, Israel, 1971

Chapter 1

Raphael da Costa

Lisbon to London, 1746

'A todos nossas irmaos presos pela Inquisicao'
'For all our brethren taken by the Inquisition.'
Portuguese prayer included in the Bevis Marks Synagogue *Yom Kippur* service,
now read in Hebrew, meant today to strengthen all who suffer for their faith.

Raphael da Costa was circumcised at London's Bevis Marks Spanish and Portuguese Synagogue in April 1746. Five days later, the 21 year old married his wife Ester da Costa in a religious ceremony. Little more about this couple is known. Their tale, woven from strands of information gleaned by inference more than reference, is a genealogical leap of faith.

Jews, known for their commercial skills and capital, arrived in Britain with William the Conqueror. Because usury, lending money for interest, was a sin in the eyes of the Church, they were encouraged to become moneylenders. Over the next century, they became enormously wealthy by financing the State Treasury. As a result, their countrymen blamed them for financial oppression and the Church demonized them.

Through the reign of Henry II, small Jewish enclaves flourished in London, Winchester, Canterbury, Oxford, Cambridge and elsewhere. When Richard the Lionheart joined the Third Crusade, anti-Semitic rioting, fuelled by waves of religious fervour, erupted throughout the realm. Scores of Jews in Lynn, Lincoln, Colchester, Thetford and Ospringe were robbed, beaten, hanged, slain or forcibly baptized.

When York's small Jewish community, attacked by a mob of Crusaders, clergymen, and indebted nobles, sought refuge as they were wont, in the local castle, they were besieged. Most killed themselves or perished in the flames, rather than face forced conversion. Those who survived were slaughtered. Then the mob destroyed all Jewish records of outstanding debts.

When the Crown acquired alternate sources of revenue in the early 1200s, many Jews, forced to wear identifying badges, were not only expelled from their homes, but also compelled to erase their debtors' obligations.

In 1275, Jews were forbidden to practise usury altogether. Although they were granted trade and farming rights, as Jews, they remained ineligible to join guilds or own land. In 1290, when they could no longer support themselves nor contribute to the economy, Edward I formally ordered all the Jews of Britain to leave his kingdom forever. Their homes and valuables reverted to the Crown.

Over the next 350 years, a small number of Jews apparently visited or settled in the country clandestinely. Several were 'foreign merchants', musicians or physicians who served the Elizabethan Court.

By the mid-seventeenth century, a number of Portuguese and Spanish Jewish merchants had fled the Inquisition for London. Though passing as devout Catholics, they formed a secret congregation that worshipped in private homes. In 1655, when England and Spain waged war over South American trade, the goods of some of these merchants became subject to seizure.

Under financial duress, they revealed that they were not Catholics at all, but refugees from the Iberian Peninsula, *Sephardi* Jews.

Like many Protestants of the time, Oliver Cromwell, who ruled Britain from 1653 until 1658, believed that ingathering the dispersed of Israel (Jeremiah 23:3) would herald Christ's Second Coming. He also realized that Jewish merchants, since they maintained close ties with brethren in the Netherlands, Spain and Portugal, might prove profitable in both commerce and war.

Like most Jews, Rabbi Menassah ben Israel, a leader of Amsterdam's Jewish community, believed that ingathering the dispersed would herald the coming of the Messiah. So, in 1655, he delivered a 'Humble Addresse' to Lord Protector Cromwell, requesting that Jews residing in Britain be allowed to gather openly for worship and that others be welcomed throughout the land.

As a result, London's tiny *Sephardi* Jewish community rented, and then purchased a house on Creechurch Lane in the City of London for use as a synagogue. They also leased a plot of land at Mile End Road for 999 years, for use as a cemetery.

Although the Monarchy was restored in 1658, Jewish tolerance continued. In October 1663 – evidently on *Simchas Torah*, which celebrates both the end and the beginning of the annual *Torah* reading cycle – Christian diarist Samuel Pepys visited the Jewish Synagogue

> where the men and boys in their vayles, and the women behind a lattice out of sight; and some things stand up, which I believe is their Law, in

a press to which all coming in do bow; and at the putting on their vayles do say something, to which others that hear him do cry Amen, and the party do kiss his vayle. Their service all in a singing way, and in Hebrew. And anon their Laws that they take out of the press are carried by several men, four or five several burthens in all, and they do relieve one another; and whether it is that every one desires to have the carrying of it, I cannot tell, thus they carried it round about the room while such a service is singing. And in the end they had a prayer for the King, which they pronounced his name in Portugall; but the prayer, like the rest, in Hebrew. But, Lord! to see the disorder, laughing, sporting, and no attention, but confusion in all their service … .

In 1701, the congregation, having outgrown its premises at Creechurch, established the Spanish and Portuguese Synagogue, modelled after its sister synagogue in Amsterdam, discreetly off Bevis Marks Street. It is still active today. Furthermore, from its earliest days at Creechurch, Bevis Marks synagogue officials meticulously noted and preserved many of its congregants' birth, circumcision, marriage and death records, scores of which pre-date 1837 compulsory government registration. These were first stored in an iron safe, then archived in lidded wooden boxes like those in church parishes. Today, all records, which extend through the nineteenth century, are fully indexed and available in print, accessible to all.

The da Costa's Bevis Marks marriage record, like many others of this era, includes the notation *vindos de Portugal*, 'arrived from Portugal'. The couple were apparently New Christians, descendants of Portuguese Jews who, in the wake of massacres and persecution generations before, had converted to Roman Catholicism.

Da Costa's circumcision also speaks volumes. Although Jews traditionally circumcise their sons eight days after birth, a male circumcised during the Iberian Inquisition, which lasted from 1481 until the early 1800s, would have courted death. Yet Iberian Jewish refugees, until they underwent this rite, were not officially considered Jewish. So Bevis Marks, like the Amsterdam congregation, required that male Iberian refugees, whatever their age, be 'welcomed into the Covenant of Abraham' within two weeks of arrival.

Although payment of their ships' fares became contingent on prior agreement to speedy circumcision, many refused to comply. Some feared health consequences. Some feared that revealing their identities would compromise their international commercial interests or endanger family members left behind. Others, though they may have fled interrogation or implication in the interrogation of others, retained no ties to the faith of

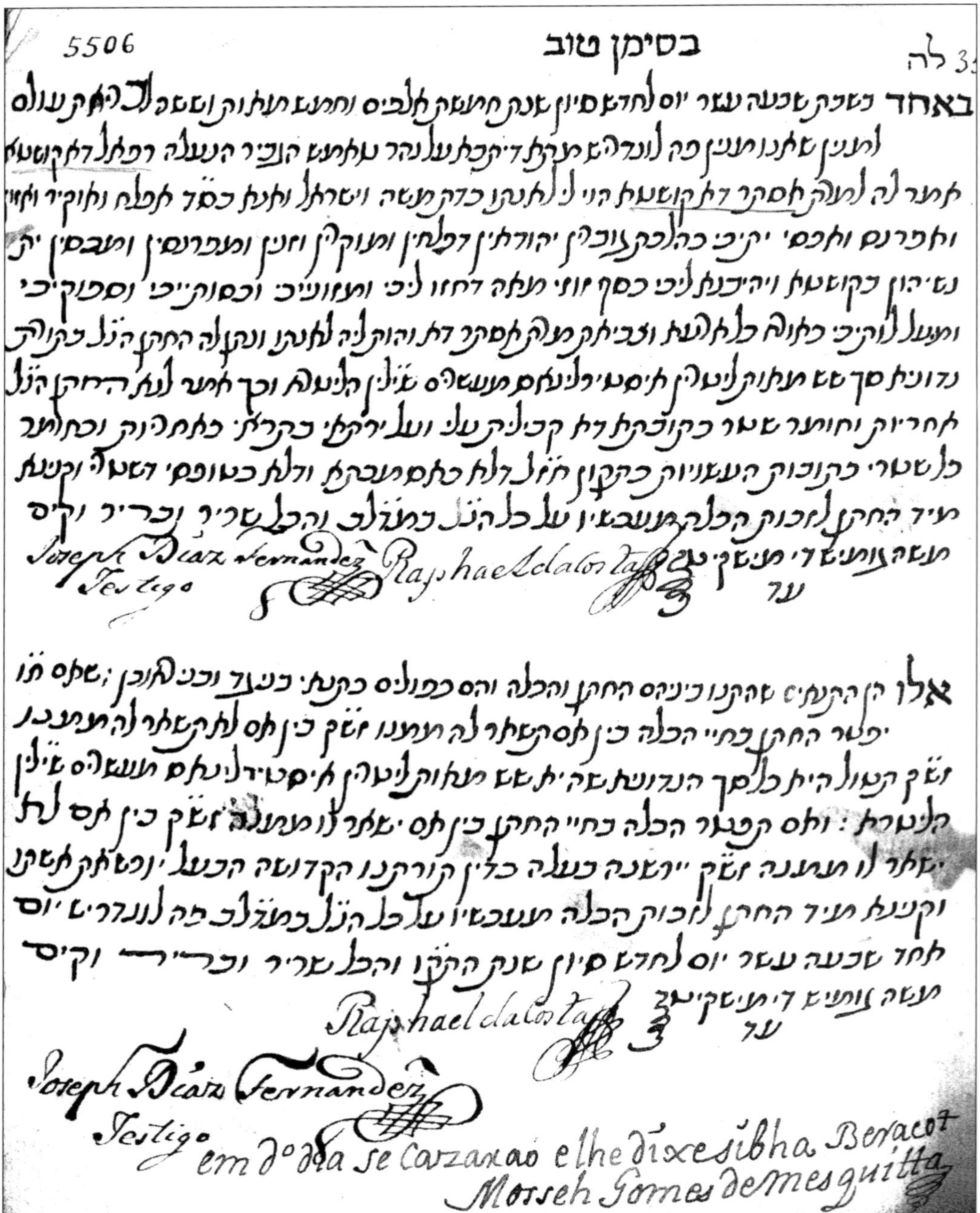
5506

בסימן טוב

לה

Joseph Diaz Fernandez
Testigo

Raphael da Costa

עד

Raphael da Costa

עד

Joseph Diaz Fernandez
Testigo

em d.o d.a se Carzarao e lhe dixe sibha Beracot
Mosseh Gomes de mesguitta

Da Costa *Ketuba, Gary Nelson and Albert Farache.*

their forefathers. So Da Costa's compliance indicated acceptance of the *Torah* and its Commandments.

The date of da Costa's circumcision reveals, by deduction, that the couple arrived in London during Passover, the Jewish holiday that commemorates the deliverance of the ancient Israelites from Egyptian slavery unto freedom. If so, they celebrated their first Festival of Freedom without fear, in freedom.

Because Raphael and Ester arrived bearing the same surname, it appears that they had previously married in the Catholic Church. To marry 'according to the laws of Moses and Israel', Bevis Marks required that Ester, like all Jewish brides, first undergo spiritual and bodily purification through ritual immersion in a *mikve*.

Contrary to Jewish custom, da Costa made no reference to his father in the traditional written marriage contract, their *ketuba*. The Bevis Marks Circumcision Register explains that

a person who returned to normal Judaism, unlike those born into the community, officially had to be regarded as fatherless, since his or her father was not deemed officially to have existed as a Jew from the strict point of view…

Many New Christian exporters, shippers, financiers and jewel merchants who had fled Iberia, maintained close commercial and personal ties with friends and family left behind. Under the auspices of Bevis Marks and in the Jewish tradition of redemption of captives, they worked to orchestrate their flights to freedom. Some refugees were able to finance their escapes with bullion, cash or diamonds. Most, however, relied on the Bevis Marks Synagogue to pay their passage on arrival.

Emigration increased in 1703, when the Methuen Treaty, by which Portuguese port-wine entered England at a favourable tariff in return for a similar concession on English woollens, was effected. To implement this agreement, Lisbon Port was declared a free zone, outside the jurisdiction of Portuguese authority. As such, it was also beyond the reach of the Inquisitors.

This had profound implications for Portuguese New Christians. If they could reach the bustling port in safety, they could flee the country. To understand the difficulty in reaching Lisbon port, one must explore Raphael and Ester da Costas's troubled, *Sephardi* heritage.

Sephardi Jews follow the same tenets and beliefs as Jews the world round. Their choice of prayers, however, as well as their order, text and melodic cantillations, form a specific liturgical tradition that differs markedly from that of Jews originating elsewhere. Many other *Sephardi* customs, like laying phylacteries, reading from the *Torah* and holiday observance, are distinctive as well. Until recent years, *Sephardi* Jews, unlike most of their European brothers, spoke a derivative of Old Castilian and Old Portuguese spiced with bits of Hebrew, Aramaic and Arabic. In light of their illustrious history and culture, as well as the suffering they endured to maintain their faith, *Sephardi* Jews are often considered the nobility of Judaism.

Jewish settlement of the Iberian Peninsula, which may date back to the time of King Solomon, increased markedly after Rome's destruction of Jerusalem. Through subsequent barbarian conquests, the community also fared well. When the Visigoths converted to Catholicism, however, they faced either baptism or expulsion. Then all, baptized or not, were threatened with slavery and distribution among Christians as gifts. So many began practising their faith in secret.

Jewish life improved dramatically from 711, under Moorish rule. For the next few golden centuries, Jews flourished in a wide variety of fields, including philosophy, mathematics, astronomy, medicine, literature and religious studies. Many were merchants, craftsmen, jugglers, music masters, royal minters and more. Some even served as ambassadors, envoys or statesmen.

In 1066, however, when a Jewish official in Granada, the Moorish capital, was accused of treason, an enraged mob stormed the royal palace and crucified him. Then, within a single day, they massacred nearly all of Granada's Jews, 4,000 souls. This marked the first Jewish persecution under Moorish rule.

As Moorish persecution increased, Jews often sought refuge in Christian strongholds. Initially, their diplomatic, monetary and linguistic skills, useful in times of war, stood them well. In the meantime, Iberia's northern Christian kingdoms launched a Reconquista, a military effort to expel the Moorish infidels that would last nearly 800 years. Through the early 1300s, periods of Jewish prosperity alternated with periods of harsh taxation, social restrictions and persecution. Each time the Jews became wealthy landowners, public officials, moneylenders and royal tax collectors, they earned the animosity of their Christian neighbours anew.

By 1391, the Jewish community faced extensive anti-Jewish legislation, along with rioting, pillage and massacres. Again thousands began practising Judaism in secret. Others embraced Catholicism, becoming New Christians.

New Christians often rose to positions of power and influence through intermarriage with Old Christians, people with ancestors born Roman Catholic. Over time, some even rose in the Church hierarchy, becoming priests, friars or nuns. Many Old Christians, however, despised New

Maniera di bruciare quelli che furono condannati dalla Inquisizione

'Way to burn those who were condemned by the Inquisition'. *http://commons. wikimedia.org/wiki/File:Rogo_inquisizione_iberica.jpg Wikipedia, public domain*

Christians more than they did the Jews. After all, they reasoned, only deceitful, dishonourable cowards would abandon their faith so easily. They despised 'Judaizers', New Christians who practised Judaism secretly, even more.

In 1478 King Ferdinand and Queen Isabella established the Spanish Inquisition to ferret out and punish all non-Catholics, especially Judaizing New Christians. After consolidating Spain under Catholic rule in 1492, they ordered all its Jews to either convert to Catholicism or face banishment.

Simon Morata, while confined in the cells of the Spanish Inquisition, bore witness.

'Death to the Jews!' …. The cry was uttered by one and was immediately taken up, and like a straw taken up by a mighty wind and tossed in the air it was tossed from mouth to mouth … . Breathless and cowed, I swayed with the crowd and was forced to witness the demoniacal act which will persist in my mind's eye until the end of my days. I saw the rotund figure of Benjamin Venal, a druggist, appear at the door of his shop … . He shouted, cursed, and fought madly … and then suddenly I saw a long knife rise up above him … and then swept swiftly down … . Then, still entangled in the crowd, I … watched the headless corpse of Venal dragged through the streets and finally deposited on a great bonfire in the Plaza de San Francisco, where it was consumed …

Rather than endanger their lives, rather than forsake their homes, thousands of Jews willingly forsook their faith. More than 100,000 others, seeking safe haven and religious freedom, fanned out across the Mediterranean. Hundreds of thousands more, those who feared sea journeys, failed to book passage, or lived inland, joined Jewish communities in neighbouring Portugal. The Portuguese spoke a similar tongue, followed similar customs, and, in the past, had provided refuge from Spanish persecutions. If Spain's harsh edict were repealed, they reasoned, they could easily return to their homes and the graves of their ancestors. Payment of a poll-tax allowed these Jews to tarry in Portugal for eight months, after which John II provided ships for those wishing to journey onward.

When their vessels reached the high seas, however, their crews, after ravishing the women aboard, threw everyone into the deep. Back in Portugal, many Jews were sold into slavery. Thousands of their children, torn from their arms, were exiled to certain death in the jungles of the tiny, newly-discovered island, Sao Tome, off the coast of Africa.

In 1497 Portuguese King Manuel I, influenced by Ferdinand and Isabella, decreed that his country's remaining Jews either convert or face expulsion. He quickly realized, however, that the sudden loss of so many professionals and craftsmen would greatly weaken the Portuguese economy. So to persuade them to stay, he had their children torn from their homes and forcibly baptized. Still, all practising Jews prepared to leave. As the date of their expulsion approached, Manuel ordered all to assemble at a central square in Lisbon. When all 20,000 had arrived, relates historian Samuel Usque, instead of boarding ships,

Dragging some by their legs and others by their hair and beards, punching and mauling them, [the king's men] brought them to the churches, where the waters of baptism were thrown upon them. Many resisted valiantly; one father covered his six sons with their prayer-shawls, exhorted them sagely to die for their faith, and killed them one by one, taking his own life last. One couple hanged themselves, and those who tried to take their bodies away for burial were slain by the enemies' spears. There were many who threw themselves into wells and others hurled themselves out of windows and were dashed to pieces … . As a result of this violence, contrary to divine and human laws, the bodies of many Jews were made Christian, but no stain ever touched their souls.

After this mass conversion, all public Jewish rites, symbols and ceremonies were immediately replaced by Catholic ritual. Many New Christians, succumbing to economic, social pressure, or pangs of love or fear, embraced their adopted faith wholeheartedly. Others secretly cleaved to their faith, yet not to the same degree. Some observed nothing outwardly, yet remained Jewish in their hearts. Some observed only what was safe and convenient. Others observed as much as they could whenever they could as best they could.

Many of those familiar with Jewish rites and ceremonies, initially intoned the prayers and followed the customs of their forefathers in secret. As one generation followed another, however, links with formal Judaism and tradition weakened considerably. Religious cornerstones, along with subtleties of the Law and complexities of observance, gradually faded from collective memory.

Jewish women, who traditionally bear responsibility for educating the next generation, eventually assumed many of the roles of male religious leaders. When youngsters reached the age of understanding, for example, their mothers introduced them to family celebrations, rituals and periodic fasts that were often integral parts of New Christian, or *converso,* practice. Yet lacking Hebrew scholarship, everyone's prayers, which were transmitted orally, became increasingly shorter, disorganized and distorted.

By following the seasons and the stages of the moon, *conversos* were able to reckon dates of major Jewish holidays, like the Day of Atonement and Passover. To preclude discovery, however, they often celebrated them a few days before or after their actual occurrence, in the bosom of their families. Occasionally, they braved peril, meeting in windowless, subterranean hideaways for communal worship.

Conversos baptized at birth often blended their new faith with the old. While outwardly saying novenas and lighting candles like Catholics, many, in their heart of hearts, actually commemorated the souls of Jewish ancestors or those who had been martyred. Some prayed for heavenly intervention to Saints Abraham, Isaac and Jacob.

Yet, writes Jewish history professor Miriam Bodian, since they

had not themselves betrayed Judaism through conversion, and since in any case they took daily risks and made enormous sacrifices to maintain a Jewish identity, they did not usually feel that their level of Jewish knowledge and observance – however rudimentary and folkloristic – was less than admirable. What their Jewishness lacked in organic connection to historic Judaism, it made up for in its steadfastness in the face of systematic persecution.

Indeed, because Portuguese *conversos* had been baptized as a group and were encouraged to marry within it, their community remained intact over generations. Shared phrases, word codes, references and actions helped identify other members of 'The Nation'. Sharing a common heritage, faith and a deadly secret life united and strengthened their community further. Yet, explains Frederic David Mocatta,

> suspicion [of Judaizing] was so easily aroused, that no man felt safe from the detractions of the servants of his household, from secret enemies, or from unguarded friends. The utmost caution hardly secured the New Christians from the suspicion of showing signs of a tendency towards Judaism. Their habits, dress, and especially diet, were carefully noted down; their abstention from or manner of performing any Catholic rite, their conduct on Jewish sabbaths and festivals, their very looks and gestures were diligently watched, and often the slightest unintentional action was reported on, and the grim familiars of the Holy Court were heard knocking at the door, ready to carry off their unsuspecting victim to its dungeons for months, for years, perhaps for ever.
>
> Thus passed on generation after generation of secret Jews, mingling with every grade of society, and filling every office of the State, and more especially of the Church, living in constant fear and trembling, still steadfast in heart, and from time to time yielding their steady tribute to the dungeon and the stake.

Enquiries at Portugal's National Torre do Tombo Archives have not revealed Inquisitional proceedings against either Raphael or Ester da Costa. Nor have their birth, parentage or Catholic marriage records come to light. Moreover, their surname, then quite common in Portugal, was used by countless, unrelated New and Old Christian families from differing geographical and social origins.

Raphael and Ester probably fled Lisbon with British merchants who, plying the Lisbon-London sea route, had been clandestinely contracted to sail them to safety. Since *conversos* were baptized Catholics, the Portuguese Inquisition could hardly question their religion. They initially charged that these 'escapees and fugitives from justice', however, owed the State money. In 1750, *Gentleman's Magazine,* for example, reveals that

> Captain Veal of the Queen of Portugal, employed in the trade, some time ago carry'd over to England some wealthy Jews, who pretended to be catholics, in order to avoid the search of the inquisition; on his return, they had him clapt up in prison for depriving them of their booty [for] they seldom fail to squeeze the rich Jews tho' converts.

Despite risks like these, British merchants, who were overwhelmingly Protestant, had little sympathy for the Catholic Inquisition.

Yet no record of the couple's arrival to London has been found. Neither Bevis Marks records, The Admiralty, the Port of London Authority, HM Customs and Excise, nor the London Metropolitan Archives hold ship accounts from this era.

Perhaps Raphael and Ester, like many Portuguese Jews, travelled under assumed names rather than endanger those they left behind. Perhaps British sea merchants kept secrets secret. Perhaps their arrival records, if they existed at all, simply did not survive.

Once in Britain, the da Costa's masted sailing ship probably threaded its way up London's main shipping lane, the Thames. Since international economic trade was booming, boats, barges, and thousands of small vessels with furled sail crowded the harbour. Outbound ones laden with woollens, grain and coal, edged inbound ones packed with furs, sugar, rum, tobacco, gemstones, spices and tea.

The couple likely settled in the close-knit, *Sephardi* community near Petticoat Lane, within walking distance of Bevis Marks Synagogue.

Since they were used to ornate Catholic churches, they may have found the synagogue's low-hanging lamps, rounded windows, timbered walls, and dark oak pews quite restrained. They may have been impressed, however, by its sanctity – its flickering 'eternal lamp' and its many *Torah* scrolls, above which the Ten Commandments glowed in gilt Hebrew script.

The da Costas' introduction to formal Judaism had begun with circumcision, ritual immersion and re-marriage. Study of Hebrew, the blessings, prayers, laws, beliefs and practices undoubtedly followed, which eased their transition from a secretive to an open Jewish society. Since *conversos* sometimes vacillated between Christianity and Judaism, however, full conformation to Orthodox rabbinical and traditional dictates and customs was mandatory.

Bevis Marks' board of directors, its *Mahamad,* maintained tight control over the social and religious lives of its congregants through a strict body of laws called *ascamot*. Only Portuguese or Spanish males over the age of 21 could become full members. Although widows and single women might be admitted as 'singles', no official provision was made for married women.

Members could not marry, divorce, refuse a synagogue function or sue fellow members without the consent of the *Mahamad*. Neither could they print a political or religious work, like a Spanish translation of the Daily Prayer Book, without permission. Neglecting to vote in synagogue elections, meeting privately for prayer, partaking of non-*kosher* food, visiting Iberia, mislaying the *ascamot* book, or opposing any of the *Mahamad*'s litany of laws earned censures or fines.

Depending on the severity of their transgressions, the *Mahamad* might deny wayward members synagogue honours, communal worship, or even the right to shave for specific lengths of time. If repentance was not forthcoming, sinners were sometimes excommunicated or denied the right to Jewish ritual burial. In time, as their decrees became less effective, the *Mahamad* appealed to secular authorities to enforce them.

During *Purim*, Jewish congregations read aloud the Book of Esther, retelling the deliverance of the Jewish people from destruction in ancient Persia. Each time the name Haman, its arch-villain, is heard, everyone blots it out with a frenzy of clapping, stamping and whirring noisemakers. But soon after the da Costas' arrival, relates Albert Hyamson, the Bevis Marks *Mahamad* expressed distress at

'the custom on the part of the more religiously exuberant section of the Congregation to create such a din at every mention of Haman's name as to shock and annoy the more moderate members'.

This said, those who could not refrain from beating on kettle-drums or clanging hammers were summarily ejected from the Synagogue by a pair of English constables, and then fined.

To their credit, and in the Biblical tradition of caring for the needy, the *Mahamad* donated all monetary revenues to Bevis Marks' orphanage, schools, hospital and almshouse. The *Mahamad* also supported a Poor Girls' Dowry Society and a Good Will Society, which, along with providing free loans to congregants, arranged apprenticeships for youngsters of the congregation.

Da Costa's occupation, like most details of his life, remains unknown. Because Jews were forbidden to open retail shops within the City of London, many sought other livelihoods. Refugee women, skilled in embroidery, often worked at home. Their husbands, if proficient in English, often became agents, book-keepers, warehousemen, brokers, clerks, public notaries or legal scriveners. Others became tailors, diamond cutters, pencil makers, glass engravers or watchmakers. Many, for a handful of shillings, purchased small stocks of portable items like pens and ink, fine-ground spectacles, pack-thread, dried rhubarb, ribbons, belt buckles, or buttons, which they peddled beyond the City walls. Perhaps da Costa hawked Spanish chestnuts, Barcelona Philberts, or Seville oranges and lemons, delicacies redolent of home. Perhaps, like many other Jewish newcomers, he hawked old clothes at Petticoat Market, an area named for the petticoats and lace once sold there by French Huguenot weavers who had fled French Catholic persecution. Though the old clothes trade thrived, writes Todd M. Endelman, it

> suffered from a very bad reputation. Jewish old-clothes men were to be met in streets and squares throughout London, in both the East and West Ends of the metropolis, for the character of the trade required that they buy from the rich, or the servants of the rich, and

Rocque's 1741 map of London, the most detailed of its time. *Wikipedia, public domain http://en.wikipedia.org/wiki/File:Rocque%27s_Map_of_London_1741-5.jpg*

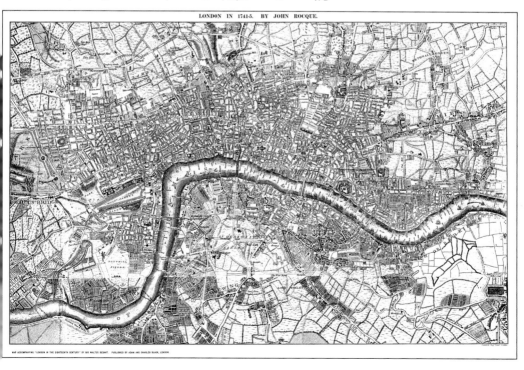

sell to the poor. In the morning hours they set forth from the East End to trudge the streets of middle-class and aristocratic London, shouting 'Old clothes' repeatedly in order to attract the attention of servants with their masters' cast-off clothes to sell … .

No matter where work took them, however, the new immigrants must have found London life oppressive. Black, sooty clouds, by-products of coal-produced light and heat, filled the air. Metal-wheeled, horse-drawn carriages clanged along narrow cobblestone streets, while large, heavy, creaky shop signs swung precariously overhead.

Dirty, dusty, unlit narrow alleyways, lined with crumbly hovels and shacks, reeked with the smell of wet horses and their waste, rotting garbage, decaying carcasses of man and beast and streams of raw sewage. Dysentery, diarrhoea, and a host of other diseases bred by crude sanitation, led to high mortality, especially among children.

Though City gates were eventually taken down, raised pavements replaced pebbly paths, and signs were set flush with shops, carriage ways remained potholed, ragged children roamed the streets, and screeches of iron-shod carriage wheels and the clatter of horses' hooves split the air. Widespread poverty bred crime. Abandoned children and vagrants formed gangs of thieves and pickpockets, while assaults and murders were common.

Ester and Raphael evidently had one child, born two years after their arrival. His name, Gabriel Raphael da Costa, follows the son-of form used as traditional identification in religious rites. *Sephardi* Jews often name newborns for living, as well as deceased, relatives. Did Raphael da Costa bequeath his father's name, omitted on his marriage contract, to his son?

Over the following generations, the da Costas shortened their surname to Costa. Initially, they alternated between both. Gabriel's son, born Isaac da Costa, for example, appears as 'Isaac Costa' on his circumcision record, just eight days later.

Later, when Isaac officially witnessed Bevis Marks' circumcision records and marriage contracts, he signed some as Isaac Costa, some as Isaac de Gabriel Costa, and others as Isaac de Gab' Costa. One grand, ornate flourish, 'Isaac de Costa son of Gabriel de rep and Esther', reveals his entire British ancestry.

Isaac and Gabriel, both born in London, enjoyed the same civic rights as their British neighbours. Those born abroad, however, could not hold property, own or hold shares in British sailing vessels, or engage in colonial trade without becoming citizens. To gain citizenship, all immigrants were required to swear oaths of allegiance 'upon the true faith of a Christian'. This, of course, no Jew could do.

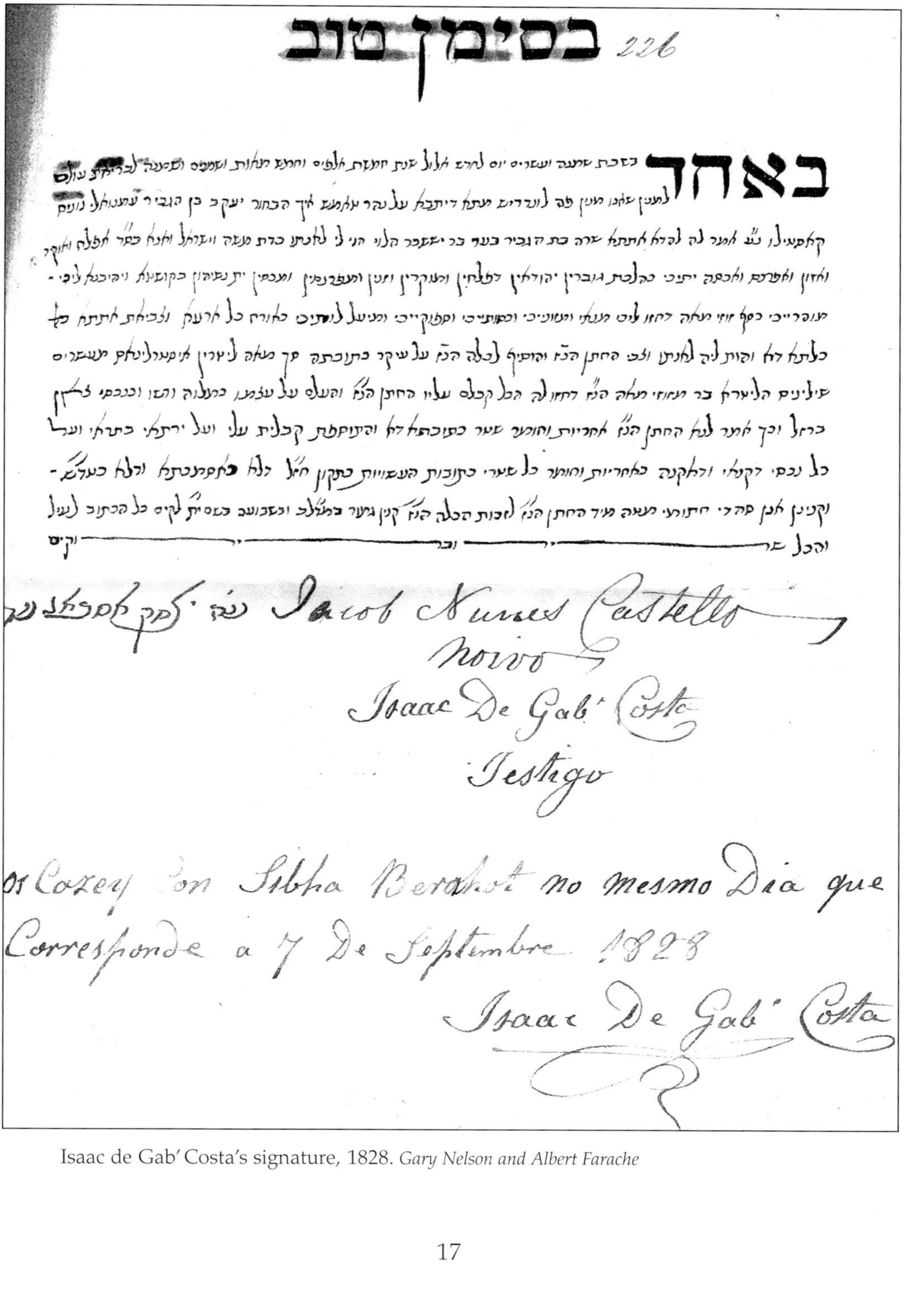

בסימן טוב 226

באהד בזכרת שמעה ועשרים יום לחדש אלול שנת חמשת אלפים וחמש מאות ושמנים ושמנה לבריאת עולם

[handwritten Hebrew ketubah text, several lines]

Jacob Nunes Castello
noivo

Isaac De Gab' Costa
Testigo

os Cazey con Sibha Berahot no mesmo Dia que
Corresponde a 7 De Septembre 1828

Isaac De Gab' Costa

Isaac de Gab' Costa's signature, 1828. *Gary Nelson and Albert Farache*

17

Because *Sephardi* Jewish merchants loyally supported the constitutional government during the Jacobite Rebellion, Parliament passed the Jewish Naturalization Act, popularly known as the 'Jew Bill of 1753', which conferred citizenship under special conditions.

A year later, however, the public, believing that the Jew Bill not only harmed English commerce and dishonoured Christianity, but also endangered the Constitution, forced its repeal. In response, many wealthy foreign-born Spanish and Portuguese Jews, their hopes for a rosier economic future dashed, embraced Christianity and, with it, full assimilation. The da Costas, however, remained true to their heritage.

Since life expectancies then were short, Raphael and Ester da Costa likely died well before 1800. Although records of their deaths do not appear in the Bevis Marks Burial Registers, they were probably laid to rest in the Spanish and Portuguese *Beit Chaim Nuevo* Cemetery off Mile End, which had served the community from 1733. After Queen Mary College purchased the site in 1974, however, thousands of remains from its oldest section, the 1734–1876 area, were re-interred in mass graves in the *Sephardi* Jewish Cemetery, Brentwood, Essex. Although authorities failed to photograph the *Nuevo* Cemetery tombstones prior to removal, they mounted memorial plaques. Today, these plaques no longer exist.

Over the years, Costa family descendants settled in Australia and the Americas, as well as across Great Britain. Even today, many bear the names Isaac, Gabriel and Raphael.

With thanks to Gary Nelson, 7th great-grandson of Raphael and Ester da Costa.

Documents

Vital Records

Gabriel Da Costa-Ester Levy, marriage contract no. 1005, 17 August 1768; Raphael da Costa-Ester da Costa 'of Portugal', marriage contract no. 713, 25 April 1746; Yaakov Nunes Castello-Sara HaLevi marriage contract no. 1710, 7 September 1828, in *Bevis Marks Records Part II: Abstracts of the Ketubot or Marriage Contracts of the Congregation from Earliest Times until 1837,* L. D. Barnett, editor, Oxford: University Press, 1940–49.

Isaac da Costa, birth entry, sheet 7, 16 December 1772, in *Bevis Marks Records Part V: the Birth Register (1767–1881) of the Spanish & Portuguese Jews' Congregation,* M. Rodrigues-Pereira and C. Loewe, London: Spanish and Portuguese Jews' Congregation, 1993.

Isaac Costa, circumcision entry no. 1404, 23 December 1772; Raphael da Costa, circumcision entry no. 673, 20 April 1746; R. D. Barnett, editor, Miriam Rodrigues-Pereira, compiler, in *Bevis Marks Records Part IV: The circumcision register of Isaac and*

Abraham de Paiba (1715-1775), London: Spanish and Portuguese Jews' Congregation: Jewish Historical Society of England, 1991.

Correspondence
Email, 31 March 2010, Luís Filipe Marques da Gama to Paul Blakely, referencing the National Torre do Tombo Archives, Portuguese, translated through Google Translations.

Bibliography

Abraham, Arthur K., 'The Testament of a Martyr [Simon Morata]', *Jewish Caravan*, Leo W. Schwarz, editor, New York: Farrar & Rinehart, 1935, 254–65.

Barnett, R. D. and W. M. Schwab, *The Sephardi Heritage: Essays on the History and Cultural Contribution of the Jews of Spain and Portugal*. Grendon, England: Gibraltar Books, 1989.

Bodian, Miriam, *Dying in the Law of Moses*. Bloomington & Indianapolis, Indiana: Indiana University Press, 2007.

Bodian, Miriam, 'Men of the Nation: The Shaping of Converso Identity in Early Modern Europe', *Past & Present*, no. 143, May 1994: 48–76.

Gitlitz, David M., *Secrecy and Deceit: The Religion of the Crypto-Jews*. Philadelphia and Jerusalem: The Jewish Publication Society, 1996.

Gubbay, Lucien and Abraham Levy, *The Sephardim*: *Their Glorious Tradition From the Babylonian Exile to the Present Day*. London: Carnell Limited, 1992.

Hyamson, Albert, *The Sephardim of England: A History of the Spanish and Portuguese Jewish Community, 1492–1951*. London: Methuen & Co. Ltd, 1951.

Kaplan, Yosef, 'Wayward New Christians and Stubborn New Jews: The Shaping of a Jewish Identity', *Jewish History*, vol. 8, nos.1–2, 1994: 27–41.

Kurinsky, Samuel, 'The da Costas: A Remarkable Sephardic Family, Fact Paper 41. http://www.hebrewhistory.info Retrieved 3 April 2010.

Lindo, E. H., *The History of the Jews of Spain and Portugal*. New York: Burt Franklin, 1848 (reprinted 1970).

Mocatta, Frederic David, *The Jews of Spain and Portugal and the Inquisition*. New York: Cooper Square, Inc., 1973.

Nathan, David, 'Costa Fascination: One of England's Oldest Jewish Families', *Avotaynu: The International Review of Jewish Genealogy*, vol. 23, no.1, Spring 2007: 28–9.

Pepys, Samuel, *The Diary of Samuel Pepys, 1663*. London: George Bell & Sons, 1893. http://www.gutenberg.org Retrieved 18 March 2010.

Roth, Cecil, *A History of the Marrano*. New York: Jewish Publication Society, 1959, 268–9.

Roth, Cecil, 'The Religion of the Marranos', *The Jewish Quarterly Review*, vol. XXII, no.1, July 1931:1–33.

Sachar, Howard M., *Farewell Espana: The World of Sephardim Remembered*. New York: Alfred A. Knopf, 1994.

Samuel, Edgar, *At the End of the Earth: Essays on the History of the Jews of England and Portugal*. London: Jewish Historical Society of England, 2004.

Stern, Rabbi Malcolm H. FASG, 'The Marrano Diaspora', *Avotaynu, The International Review of Jewish Genealogy*, vol. 8, Spring 1992: 9–13.

Studnicki-Gizbert, Daviken, 'La Nacion Among the Nations', *Atlantic Diasporas: Jews, Conversos, and Crypto-Jews in the Age of Mercantilism, 1500–1800*, Richard L. Kagan and

Philip D. Morgan, editors. Baltimore: The Johns Hopkins Press, 2009, 75– 84.

Urban, Sylvanus, 'Foreign Advices', *Gentleman's Magazine,* vol. XX, March 1750:142. http://www.bodley.ox.ac.uk Retrieved 11 March 2011.

Usque, Samuel, 'Consolation for the Tribulations of Israel', *The Expulsion: 1492 Chronicles,* David Raphael, editor. North Hollywood: Carmi House Press, 1992, 135–44.

Wolf, Lucien, editor, *Menasseh ben Israel's Mission to Oliver Cromwell: Being a Reprint of the Pamphlets Published by Menasseh ben Israel to Promote the Re-admission of the Jews to England, 1649–1656,* 1901. London: Jewish Historical Society, Macmillan. www.archive.org Retrieved 6 April 2010.

Chapter 2

Isaac Michael Myers

Amsterdam, The Netherlands to London, 1824

*The righteous shall flourish like the palm-tree; he shall grow
like a cedar in Lebanon.*
Psalm 92:13.

M oses and Sarah Myers left Amsterdam for London, either aboard a small sail-powered packet ship or a faster, tall-masted clipper ship, in 1824. Since the North Sea was especially stormy that year, their trip, which may have taken weeks, was probably memorable for their children, Isaac Michael, 9, and Eva, 2. It was probably trying for their mother, however. Sarah Myers was pregnant.

Yet she must have been in fine spirits. Although various sources place her birth in 1789, 1791, and 1792, they all agree on one point. Sarah, the daughter of Shmuel Cohen, was London-born. She was returning home.

The Jews of Amsterdam and London, though separated by a wide expanse of water, were closely connected in spirit. From the 1500s onwards, Amsterdam had offered safe haven to *Sephardi* Jews fleeing the Inquisition. During the following century, the city offered waves of penniless *Ashkenazi* Jews, descendants of medieval communities that originated along the Rhine River, refuge. Some fled the recurring unrest and violence of the Thirty Years War. Others fled the Chmielnicki Uprising, which, at the hands of Russian Orthodox Cossacks and Ukrainian peasants, left 100,000 – if not more – Jews dead.

Although Amsterdam's *Ashkenazi* refugees spoke Yiddish and followed Eastern European religious practice, they initially joined existent *Sephardi* congregations. As their numbers grew, however, the *Sephardi* hierarchy became increasingly reluctant to support them or 'defile' their ranks through intermarriage. *Sephardi* marriage contracts routinely labelled *Ashkenazi* brides as *Tedescos* (Germans), or more pointedly, left them nameless. Finally, in

1635, Amsterdam's *Ashkenazi* community established a synagogue of its own led by religious leaders from their countries of origin.

Ashkenazi refugees also poured into London, creating close-knit communities in the East End, an area previously settled by Huguenots and other immigrants. They initially attended the *Sephardi* synagogue at Creechurch Lane, burying their dead at the Spanish and Portuguese cemetery at Mile End.

The Glorious Revolution of 1688–89, which united Britain and The Netherlands, led to improved communication and reciprocal trade between the two countries. Because Amsterdam also maintained close ties with Hamburg, enterprising German *Ashkenazi* Jews reached London as well.

By the following year, London's growing *Ashkenazi* community established the Great Synagogue, a 'daughter' of Amsterdam's *Ashkenazi* congregation, at Duke's Place, Aldgate, East End. Six years later, they acquired a cemetery of their own. As their numbers grew, their characteristic pronunciation of Hebrew, traditions and use of Yiddish eventually supplanted the area's *Sephardi* character.

Because the London and Amsterdam *Ashkenazi* Jewish communities were so closely related, arranged marriages between them were not uncommon. When these occurred, reciprocal visits, though difficult and expensive, naturally followed. Indeed, some census records note Jewish Londoners 'visiting' Amsterdam and Amsterdam Jews 'visiting' London.

Michael Myers's father, Moses, born in 1787, was evidently the son of Asser Marcus Myer Nikkelsberg. Jewish males are traditionally identified by the son-of form, personal names followed by the names of their fathers. So Asser Marcus, within his community, would have been known as Asser Marcus [son-of] Myer. 'Nikkelsberg', a town in southern Moravia (today in the Czech Republic), evidently indicated his place of origin. Moses, who was eventually born in Amsterdam, dropped 'Nikkelsberg' altogether. Following tradition, however, he retained the name of his father, Myer, albeit it in the possessive form, becoming Moses Myers.

During the Dutch Republic, 1581 to 1795, many Amsterdam Jews, tolerated but excluded from craft guilds, worked as unskilled labourers. Although the Industrial Revolution was sweeping much of Europe, The Netherlands continued to suffer general economic decline, with trade, shipping, fishing and small businesses remaining stagnant.

Moses and Sarah Myers, who likely reached London seeking economic opportunity, probably settled among Dutch Jews living in the Houndsditch area, City of London. Moses may have initially peddled trinkets or, like many other Dutch immigrants, rolled cigars or sold used clothes. Todd M. Endelman writes that hundreds of old clothes dealers fanned out each day through the streets and squares of middle-class and aristocratic London to purchase articles now deemed unfashionable or too worn by their owners. In Rag Fair an open-air market held daily in Rosemary Lane, near Tower Hill, Jewish dealers purchased the used goods collected earlier and offered them for sale to the hundreds of customers who jammed the area, making it at times nearly impassable.

Elizabeth, the Myers's third child, was born within months of arrival in London, with Julia and Kate following within the next two years. In the meantime, Michael, their older brother, was probably studying Hebrew and the basics of Judaism in *cheder*. After his *Bar Mitzva* in 1828, he may have transferred to the Jews' Free School, which had originally been the Great Synagogue's *Talmud Torah*. This esteemed institution implemented rote learning through the monitor system, whereby older students, coached by master teachers, instructed younger ones. According to Cecil Roth in *History of the Great Synagogue,*

> … owing to the paucity of elementary schoolbooks, [youngsters] learned the shape of the letters from a rotating disc, while they practised writing by tracing the letters with their forefingers in a trough of silver sand, which could be smoothed over ready for the next attempt.

Because most students arrived illiterate in English, the Free School, besides providing a haven from the violence and crime on the streets, also facilitated their assimilation.

In 1892, Israel Zangwill, once himself a student there, recalled that

> the bell of the great Ghetto school, summoning its pupils from the reeking courts and alleys, from the garrets and the cellars, [called] them to come and be Anglicized. And they came in a great straggling procession recruited from every lane and by-way, big children and little children, boys in blackening corduroy, and girls in washed-out cotton; tidy children and ragged children; children in great shapeless boots gaping at the toes; sickly children, and sturdy children, and diseased children; bright eyed children and hollow eyed children; quaint sallow foreign looking children, and fresh coloured English looking children … all hastening at the inexorable clang of the big school bell.

Michael apparently excelled in his studies. Part of a small group of 'precociously-learned' boys, he won the esteem of Dr Solomon Herschell, rabbi of the Great Synagogue and 'Chief Rabbi of the German and Polish Jews in England'. Indeed, Michael may have learned to read directly from the *Torah*, no mean achievement, under his tutelage. Since needy Jews often accosted the wealthy and influential in their homes, businesses, and on the streets, he may have also witnessed the rabbi distributing charity.

Congregants of the Great Synagogue, heeding the Biblical injunction to care for the needy, had long supplied dowries to indigent brides and supported religious schools. They also maintained a Soup Kitchen, a Bread, Meat and Coal Charity, a Five Shilling Sabbath Charity, a Ladies' Benevolent Institution, a Society for Clothing Poor Jewish Boys, and an Institution for the Relief of the Indigent Blind of the Jewish Persuasion. Cecil Roth notes that these charities

> were administered in the conventional fashion of the time, with occasional meetings of subscribers at the City taverns, anniversary dinners for the purpose of raising funds, and gargantuan libations of wine and spirits (from which the Readers and Beadles of the synagogues were, 'from particular reasons', carefully excluded). Moreover, when the benefits available were not sufficient for all the applicants, lots were drawn, specially made lottery-wheels being used for the purpose.

London's long-established Anglo-Jewish community, beyond fulfilling its religious obligations and expressing genuine feelings of compassion, had another motive for supporting the needy.

Many new arrivals, disoriented by city life, unskilled, illiterate in English, and living by their wits alone, were drawn to the shady world between legal and illegal pursuits. Poverty-stricken women, for example, sometimes turned to prostitution. Innkeepers ran brothels. Traders often dealt in stolen goods, hawkers passed counterfeit coins and salesmen peddled trinkets as valuables. According to an anonymous contributor to *The Edinburgh Journal* in 1848, all Jews, even those living in Britain for generations, were coarse, dirty, uncultured, unshorn criminals, 'bargaining and disputing in that harsh, snivelling Jewish accent…'

No wonder Anglo-Jews offered monetary assistance to the newcomers, hoping it would foster British manners, morals and respectability. To assure them productive futures, they also arranged tailoring, shoe-making, cabinet-making and hat-making apprenticeships for boys and housework, needlework and cooking apprenticeships for girls.

Rejected 'on account of his youth insignificant and diminutive figure'. *Minutes, Burial Society Committee of the Great Synagogue, 1840*

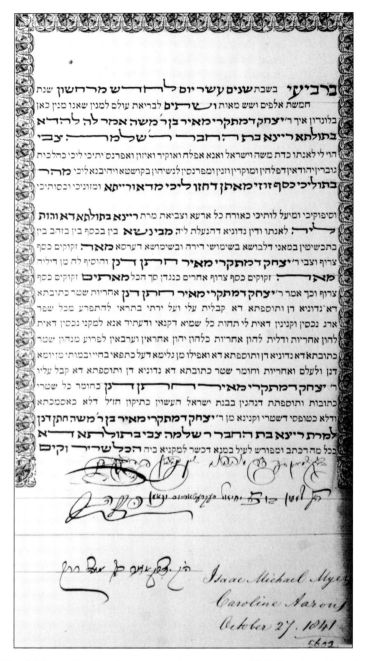

Isaac Michael Myers-Caroline Aarons marriage contract, 1841, London. Great Synagogue, from *Marriage Records of the Great Synagogue, London, 1791–1885*, Harold and Miriam Lewin

Sometimes the needy established charitable organizations on their own. Roth relates, for example, that when Cholera Morbus struck London's East End in 1832,

> A poor cucumber-seller, Abraham Green, whose sense of pity was aroused, left his stall and went round the streets and private houses and shops in the Jewish quarter to find help. Carrying two of [his] children in his arms and leading the third by the hand, he appealed to his warm-hearted coreligionists until he had collected in his cucumber-bowl the nucleus of a maintenance fund. This was the origin of the Jews' Orphan Asylum, which maintained, clothes, educated, and apprenticed Jewish orphan children.

Although Jews succumbed more often to malignant agues, remittent fevers, smallpox and influenza than cholera, John Hogg MD observed that

> This dreadful disease, most insidious in its invasion, most rapid in its progress, and most fatal in its attack, spares neither youth nor age, sex nor constitution, rich nor poor. ... in some places the patients were bled, in others dependence was placed on saline medicines; some practitioners employed stimulants, and others the hot bath; in short every drug in the materia medica was canvassed, in the hope of giving relief to the miserable sufferers.

Michael evidently became inured to the East End's suffering and death from an early age. In 1840 he applied to join the Burial Society of the Great Synagogue. Its members ritually cleansed bodies of the deceased, wrapped them in white linen shrouds, then arranged their burials, in simple, wooden coffins, as soon as possible. Burial Society members, wondering if one so young could deal with the grim reality of mortality and aware that strength to lift bodies and dig graves was crucial, refused Myers's application twice over, 'on account of his youth, insignificant and diminutive figure'. Youth would pass. But there was no denying Myers's unusually short stature.

Although a number of sources refer to 'little Mr Myers' or Myertje, a Dutch diminutive, none reveals the cause of his abbreviated height. Myers's obituary, however, notes that he 'was called upon at a very early age to fight hard in the battle of life'. Whether he suffered a birth defect or some harsh illness in his youth, Myers's lack of physical stature evidently strengthened his heart and softened his soul toward the plight of others.

By 1841, the Myers family moved to High Street, Shadwell, on the River Thames, a rough area pocked with wharves, shipyards and associated industries. There they ran a slops shop, selling cheap, off-the-peg, loose-fitting seamen's clothes. Moses Myers, to supplement their income, also hand manufactured black-lead pencils.

The British wrote with quills and ink until the 1550s. Because black graphite, discovered in Borrowdale, Cumbria, was believed to be a form of lead, it was dubbed 'black-lead'. Since graphite sticks alone were too brittle for writing, they were originally covered with bits of sheepskin or stiffened with tightly-looped string. By the 1840s, however, lead-pencil manufacturers had learned to compress graphite powder into solid sticks instead, inserting them between two grooved wooden halves, then gluing them together. The official catalogue of The 1851 Great Exhibition, Hyde Park, London, informs artists, architects and engineers that their 'Purified Lead Pencils, Perfectly Free From Grit, May be Entirely Erased, and Will Maintain a Firm Point'.

Myers wed London-born Caroline, daughter of Solomon and Mary Aarons, in 1841, then set up house at Mitre Street, Duke's Place, Aldgate, near the Great Synagogue. While he worked as 'a schoolmaster and teacher of Hebrew', possibly in a *cheder* or at the nearby Jews' Free School, Caroline evidently helped her father in his Hebrew bookshop. Their first child, Henry Solomon, arrived within the year.

By 1845, Jewish leaders, in addition to fulfilling the physical needs of the poor, were concerned with their spiritual needs. Aware that Jews removed from tradition might be tempted by secular life and even (heaven forefend) by Christianity, they established the General Literary and Scientific Institute to raise their religious and cultural levels. Popularly known as Sussex Hall, this organization offered local shopkeepers, street traders and craftsmen lectures on Jewish subjects, as well as Hebrew, German and French instruction. In addition to supporting a circulating library, it also hosted art exhibitions, displays of curiosities, and concerts.

That same year, Myers applied once again for membership in the Burial Society of the Great Synagogue. For some reason, however, he withdrew his application before the vote was taken. Perhaps family duties precluded assuming such grave responsibility. Nine months to the day after their daughter Mary was born, Phoebe arrived. Asher, destined to become editor and manager of *The Jewish Chronicle,* followed two years later.

All around them, excitement was building. In 1847, Lionel de Rothschild, a pillar of Anglo-Jewish society and scion of the international Rothschild financial dynasty, was elected to the British House of Commons. As a practising Jew, however, he refused to take the oath of allegiance 'upon the true faith of a Christian'.

Lionel's father, Baron Nathan Mayer Rothschild, founder of the family's London branch, had financed Britain's struggle against Napoleon, negotiated the Irish Famine Loan, operated London's Royal Mint Refinery, and supported a wide range of philanthropic organizations. Yet, to the chagrin of the Jewish community, his son was barred from sitting in chamber.

The British House of Commons, in response, approved the Jewish Disabilities Bill, which by modifying the required oath, allowed Jews to enter Parliament. The House of Lords, however, rejected it the following year. When this bill was rejected in 1849 as well, Lionel de Rothschild resigned his seat. Although he was repeatedly re-elected until 1857, the Disabilities Bill was defeated each time it was introduced.

By 1851, the Myers were living at Duke Street, together with six children under the age of nine, three lodgers and an elderly servant. Two years later, when Michael applied again for membership in the Burial Society of the Great Synagogue, little Rosie, too, had joined the family. This time, Myers was duly elected by a wide margin of votes. For the next forty years he served as its 'burial rabbi', arranging and officiating at funerals.

Because Myers, in his official capacity, also visited the ailing and the aging, he became a faithful subscriber to the Society for the Relief of the Aged Needy, the Soup Kitchen Society and many other charitable institutions. His busy life, however, did not preclude familial obligations. Two more daughters, Esther and Emma, arrived in 1855 and 1857.

The following year, Lionel de Rothschild was finally allowed to take the Parliamentary oath with covered head in an acceptable form. For the first time, Britain's Jews had gained legislative representation.

In 1859, Myers asked the Burial Society to increase his wages, 'in consequence of the additional duties devolving upon them since the opening of the new burial ground at West Ham from the further distance of the same'. Thereafter he received a respectable addition of £10 per annum, for which he undoubtedly found good use. Caroline was expecting their tenth child, Mark.

Sussex Hall, unable to compete with livelier amusements like pubs, gambling, music halls and street entertainment, closed that same year. In its place, Myers helped found the Society for Diffusion of Jewish Knowledge, an organization that encouraged the poor to embrace their religious heritage. Their need, observed *The Jewish Chronicle* in 1860, was acute.

If anyone entertains the least doubt about the subject, he can easily convince himself by making a tour through the localities occupied by Jews on any Sabbath or festival. He will see there that the whole day is, by the vast majority, spent in frivolous amusement; that no portion is set apart for religious meditation; and, to aggravate the evil, no

Full house: ten Myers's' children, a sister, nephew, elderly lodger, and servant. *Census Returns of England and Wales, 1861.*

facilities for religious instruction are afforded even to those who are religiously inclined.

To address this situation, the Society established a Sabbath School and, to dissuade young men from frequenting public houses, coffee-houses, gambling dens, dance halls and worse, also organized Friday evening Bible classes. Over the coming years, the Society, besides offering Sabbath afternoon religious discourses, many of which Myers presented, also published simplified tracts featuring Bible stories, religious fables and descriptions of Jewish holidays and practices. Some of these included practical advice. Readers were warned, for example, to drink copious amounts of water and avoid forbidden food, for fear of disease.

In 1860, Myers insured a property at Bedford Street and Commercial Road, perhaps one of its many book and printer shops. In the meantime, Caroline, a 'Hebrew bookseller', probably continued working in Aldgate at her father's shop. By the following year, the ten children were sharing quarters with Myers's sister, nephew, an elderly lodger and a servant girl. Solomon, the eldest, worked as a clerk, while his two younger sisters sewed dresses and caps. Their younger siblings were all in school.

Five years later, Myers was appointed almoner, a religious functionary who distributed alms to the needy, to Baroness Charlotte de Rothschild. The two shared a mutual interest in one of her favourite charities, the Jews' Free School. For the next fifty years, literally until the day of his death, Myers distributed Rothschild alms with 'a rare combination of justice and tenderness'.

Baroness Charlotte de Rothschild, who had married her cousin Lionel, not only personally funded the Jews' Free School, but also founded an Invalids' Kitchen, a Home for Aged Incurables and an Emigration Society. She also presided over the Ladies' Benevolent Loan and Visiting Society. In addition to dispersing funds to the needy for over thirty years, she and her husband served on boards of many Jewish organizations, including the Board of Deputies of British Jews (under leadership of philanthropist Moses Montefiore), the Great Synagogue, the Central Synagogue, United Synagogue, the Board of Guardians for Relief of the Jewish Poor and the Anglo-Jewish Society. Indeed, writes Chaim Bermant, 'The Chief Rabbi in exercising his authority would invoke the name of Heaven: if that failed he would invoke the name of Rothschild.'

Excerpts from Charlotte de Rothschild's correspondence reveal her special relationship with Myers.

1 August 1866
In the Free School and among its two thousand children there is far less to find fault with and little Mr Myers assures me that now the vestries endeavour to do their utmosts …

27 August 1866
This morning little Mr Myers came down as a treat from Cholera-haunted Whitechapel to have his accounts settled in fresh air, and be braced and cheered by balmy zephyrs and gracefully waving trees, and sweet-smelling flowers.

Yet, noted *The Jewish Chronicle* in 1866,

The scourge [of cholera] has not fallen as heavily upon us as our neighbor. While offering up our heartfelt thanks to Him who smites and binds up the wound for the alleviation of this indication, the question naturally suggests itself, To what agency under Divine Providence are we indebted for this evident mitigation of the evil in our midst?

The Special Cholera Relief Fund of the Board of Guardians for the Relief of the Jewish Poor, probably through Rothschild largesse, distributed food and disinfectants to the ailing. In addition, The Jewish Board of Guardians also engaged inspectors to teach the poor sanitary precautions that evidently helped save lives.

London's Anglo-Jews, who largely followed orthodox belief and practice, initially attended three large, independent places of worship, the Great

Synagogue (1690), the New Synagogue (1761) and the Hambro (1707), all located within the City of London. As their circumstances improved, however, many congregants left for distant West End neighbourhoods. Because Orthodox Judaism prohibits travel on Sabbaths and the holidays, two 'daughter' synagogues, the Central (1855) and the Bayswater (1863), sprang up in their wake.

These five, the Great, New, Hambro, Central and Bayswater Synagogues, joined in 1870, to form the orthodox United Synagogue. Their union ultimately strengthened the role of Britain's Chief Rabbi, which evolved from the Rabbinate of the Great Synagogue. According to Chaim Bermant,

> The United Synagogue is based on the belief in God, the law of Moses and the adoration of most things English. Catholic in scope and Anglican in manner, it stands for Anglo-Jewry as the Church of England stands to England.

From about 1871 until the end of their lives, Michael and Caroline Myers lived in narrow Sandy's Row, Spitalfields, an area outside the City of London, within walking distance of both the Great Synagogue and Sandy's Row Synagogue, the 'Dutch Shool' (1853). Initially, six of their children, a cook, a teacher, two feather-makers and two students, were still at home.

Despite his advanced age, Myers continued to participate in the Diffusion of Jewish Knowledge Society. By 1877, observed the London-based *The Jewish Chronicle*, educational efforts like these finally bore fruit.

> Culture is advancing with great strides in the community. The rising generation takes worthily its rank by the side of the general population. And in proportion as education advances, so rises the feeling of self-respect and the general moral tone. Unstable trades and occupations hold our inducements to an unsettled life and temptations to departure from the strict path of rectitude are sensibly on the decrease, and several of them have entirely been given up.

'Path of rectitude' (Psalm 27:11), sometimes translated as 'path of righteousness', was a common phrase in the late-nineteenth century. The British considered the poor, most of whom lived in squalor and worked at marginal occupations, to be disreputable and dishonourable – and because of their growing numbers, by proxy, all Jews.

The Anglo-Jewish middle-class established the Path of Rectitude Society to counter this perception. Its members not only promoted moral integrity and righteousness among their poorer brothers, but also offered classes in *Mishnah*, a collection of early oral interpretations of Jewish Law.

On Wednesday [25 February 1880], a testimonial, consisting of a handsome silver salver, was presented to Mr I. M. Myers, by the members of the "Path of Rectitude" Friendly Society, of which Mr Myers had been the secretary for upward of thirty years.

Two years later, *The Jewish Chronicle* announced that Caroline Myers, after 'long suffering borne with patience and fortitude', died at age 63, 'deeply mourned by her sorrowing family'. She is buried in West Ham Cemetery, London.

J. M. Duparc, a grandson who used to visit Myers during school holidays, recalls,

Grandfather lived [in a] 'grace and favour' flat, owned by the Rothschilds; I imagine that he enjoyed the privilege because he was a sort of almoner for New Court [the Rothschild Bank]. The flat … was situated above … the 'Invalids' Kitchen', no doubt a Rothschild charity …. There was an overspill from … [Petticoat] Lane to Sandy's Row and I remember vividly those itinerant vendors. There was a little old man who toddled along balancing a huge glass bowl on his head. He was selling pickled Dutch cucumbers. . . . Another man trundled a little trolley; his call was ''ot pies, pies all 'ot'. A third sold sweetmeats in paper bags; he cried: 'Limes, limes!'

Myers continued his personal and public charitable endeavours. Once a week, recalls DuParc 'he sat at a table on which were piles of sovereigns, half-sovereigns and silver coins…. Long before opening time, there was a noisy crowd waiting outside for the doors to open.'

Though his sight and hearing were deteriorating, Myers, gifted *Torah* reader, inspiring prayer leader, cantor and fluent speaker, continued to play an active role in his synagogue.

Myers died in November 1898 in Sandy's Row, Spitalfields. His *The Jewish Chronicle* obituary lauds

a scholar of no mean order. He was always studying, always had a 'good thing' to impart, and was never without some learned work at hand … . His knowledge of the Bible and the Prayer Book was very great … . nothing delighted him more than to impart information to a willing listener. … His early struggles fitted him with the best of qualifications for the discharge of the sacred trust which for so many years he fulfilled with a rare combination of justice and tenderness, that of almoner for the generous benefactors of the poor … . The late Mr I.

M. Myers had held the office of sexton for upwards of half-a-century, and there was probably not a family within the united congregations which had not been brought into personal touch with him when the hand of death had fallen upon them, and carried off one of the dear ones of the family circle. We could all understand how much tact and feeling were needed in order to carry out the melancholy duties which daily devolved upon him, and yet the veteran sexton never suffered the monotonous routine of his avocation to crush out of him that sympathy and cheerfulness of disposition so needful for the successful performance of any public charge, and which was a prime qualification in one whose duty was ever among those who were depressed with grief and sorrow.'

An anonymous writer adds,

we are accustomed Sabbath by Sabbath to invoke the blessing of God upon those who occupy themselves in faithfulness with the wants of the congregation, and … a word of tribute should be heard in the synagogue when a trusted public servant who had served it well was called to his eternal rest.

With thanks to Lois Kaufman, great-great-grand-daughter of Isaac Michael and Caroline Myers.

Documents

Vital Records
Asser Marcus Meyer, Amsterdam, birth record, 1761, Akevoth.
Isaac Michael Myers, Deaths registered in October-November-December 1898, 1c.167, *England and Wales Civil Registration Indexes*, London, GRO.
Isaac Michael Myers-Caroline Aarons, marriage contract, 27 October 1841, London Great Synagogue, in *Marriage Records of the Great Synagogue, London, 1791–1885*, Harold and Miriam Lewin, Jerusalem: privately printed, 2004.
Moshe b. Potiboich-Sara Chy"bat Shmuel Cohen, marriage contract , 1813, London New Synagogue, in *New Synagogue Marriage Records 1791–1823 & 1737-1842*, Shire, Angela, transcriber, privately published, date not noted.
Mozes Asser Nikkelsburg, birth record, 8 Oct 1787;
Moshe ben Asher ben Meyer, circumcision record, 3 *Cheshvan* 5548, in *Besnijdenissen en Geboorten in Amsterdam,* 1697-1811, Jits von Straten, Akevoth.

Census records
Isaac M Myers household, HO107, 1524/72, TNA.
Isaac M Myers household, RG 9, 211/8, TNA.
Isaac M Myers household, RG10, 503/26, TNA.
Isaac M Myers household, RG11, 437/ 93, TNA.
Isaac M Myers household, RG12, 275/33, TNA.
Mars [Moses] Myers household, HO107, 703/5, TNA.

Correspondence
Letters of Charlotte de Rothschild, 1 August and 27 August 1866, 000/84, Rothschild
   Archive London.

Other
Minutes, Burial Society Committee of the Great Synagogue, London *Beit Din*, 3 August
   1840, 24 February 1845, 11 August 1853, 4 January 1859, ACC/2712/GTS/351, LMA.
Sun Life insurance policy, 1860, Isaac Michael Myers, Guildhall Library MS 11936,
   LMA.

Bibliography

Alderman, Geoffrey, *Modern British Jewry*. Oxford: Oxford University, 1998.
'Association for the Diffusion of Religious Knowledge', *The Jewish Chronicle*, 1 June 1860:5.
Bermant, Chaim, *Troubled Eden: An Anatomy of British Jewry*. New York: Basic Books, Inc.,
   1970.
Blom, J. C. H., R. G. Fuks-Mansfeld, and I. Schoffer, editors, *The History of the Jews in the
   Netherlands*. Oxford: The Littman Library of Jewish Civilization, 2007.
Chambers, Robert and William, *Edinburgh Journal*, Edinburgh: W. and R. Chambers, 1848.
   http://books.google.com Retrieved 25 April 2012.
'Death Notice', referencing Caroline Myers, *The Jewish Chronicle,* 17 February 1882: 1.
'Death of Mr. Asher I. Myers', *The Jewish Chronicle,* 16 May 1902: 7.
DuParc, J.M. 'Down Sandy's Row', *The Jewish Chronicle*, 3 October 1975: 9.
'East London Synagogue: Some Recollections, By an Old Stager', *The Jewish Chronicle,* 26
   August 1927: 6.
Ellis Robert, *Official Descriptive and Illustrated Catalogue of the Works of Industry of All
   Nations,* Part 1, Great Britain Commissioners for the Exhibition of 1851. London: W.
   Clowes & Sons, 1851 http://books.google.com/ Retrieved 14 May 2010.
Endelman, Todd M., *The Jews of Georgian England, 1714–1830: Tradition and Change in a
   Liberal Society*. Philadelphia: Jewish Publication Society, 1979.
Higgins, Robert Mcr, '1832 Cholera Epidemic in East London', East *London Record,* Issue
   2 (1979). http://www.mernick.org.uk Retrieved 15 July 2010.
Hogg, M. D., editor. *London As It is: Observations on the Health, Habits, and Amusements
   of the People.* St James' Square, London: John Macrone, 1837. http://books.google.com
   Retrieved 7 June 2010.
'Literary Matters', *The Jewish Chronicle,* 7 September 1877:11.
Maynard, Jeffrey, editor. *Anglo-Jewish Miscellanies.* http://www.jeffreymaynard.com
   Retrieved 22 March 2012.
Mayhew, Henry, *London Labour and the London Poor*, vol. II. London: Charles Griffin and
   Company, Exeter Street, Strand. http://books.google.com Retrieved 31 May 2010.

Myers, A. I., compiler, *Jewish Directory, 1874*. Details unknown, available at the Jewish Genealogical Society of Great Britain Library, London.

'Rag Fair, Petticoat-Lane: The Debatable Lands in London', author unknown, *The Builder,* 3 July 1958. http://www.mernick.org.uk Retrieved 1 June 2010.

Roth, Cecil, *History of the Great Synagogue.* London: E Goldston, 1950, The Susser Archive: Studies in Anglo-Jewish History. http://www. jewishgen.org Retrieved 12 July 2010.

Shire, Angela, *Great Synagogue Marriage Records 1791–1859, Great Synagogue Marriage Registers 1791-1850*. Crediton, Devon: Frank J. Gent, 2001.

Shire, Angela, transcriber and publisher, *New Synagogue Birth Records 1771–1864.* Details unknown.

Sonnenberg-Stern, Karina, *Emancipation and Poverty: the Ashkenazi Jews of Amsterdam, 1796–1850*. Oxford: Saint Antony's College, 2000.

'On Wednesday, a Testimonial', *The Jewish Chronicle,* 27 February 1880: 13.

'The Epidemic Among Our Poor', *The Jewish Chronicle*, 17 August 1866: 4.

'The Late Mr. I. M. Myers', *The Jewish Chronicle,* 2 December 1898:13.

Chapter 3

Ze'ev Yitzhak Dovid HaLevi

Pinczow, Congress Poland to London, 1846

'Work, Wait, Win'
Davis family motto.

By 1835, when Ze'ev Yitzhak Dovid HaLevi was born, Jews had lived in Poland for over a millennium. Despite periodic waves of anti-Semitism, they had enjoyed a large measure of religious tolerance and cultural autonomy.

Jews apparently reached Pinczow, Ze'ev's hometown near Krakow, Congress Poland, during the sixteenth century. Their relationship with the local Church and the ruling nobility waxed and waned. By 1764, though considered outsiders, Jewish butchers, bakers, jewellers, craftsmen, wine makers and shopkeepers contributed much to Pinczow's economy. So did Jewish traders, who forged commercial ties with distant Leipzig and Vienna, as well as Polish cities.

As Pinczow's Jewish community grew in size, it also grew in stature, meriting representation at the Council of the Four Lands. This autonomous Jewish parliament, which presided over communities in Greater Poland, Little Poland, Ruthenia and Volhynia between 1580 and 1764, stipulated laws, appointed rabbinical rights and dealt with other important issues.

Pinczow's Jews, more than half the town, followed a branch of orthodox, mystical Judaism born in the eighteenth century called *Hasidus*. This dynamic movement, writes Ilya Ehrenbourg, reflected a

desire for a new life – and everlasting urge to throw off the yoke of the constant fasts, ceremonials, and prayers. People were dying amidst bookish dust, amidst the complicated quibblings of the Talmud, amid such vital questions as: Is it permitted to kill a flea on the Sabbath? .... Then in a little Polish village, amid the base debaucheries of the provincial nobility, amid the dark sleep of the ignorant peasantry, amid poverty and snow, the illuminating and great philosophy of Baal Shem Tov [Isidore ben Eliezer] was born. Translated into everyday language, into the language of the village paupers, it proclaimed: 'Long live life.' And hearing these words, thousands of hearts began to beat excitedly.

Among these were 'righteous ones', disciples renown for piety and scholarship who, criss-crossing Poland and the Ukraine, taught that even unlearned Jews could reach spiritual heights through prayer, joy, love of man and love of God.

Yiddish-speaking Pinczow sent their sons, 3 to 13, to *cheder*, where they pored over religious studies eight to twelve hours a day. Even as adults, Pinczow Jews devoted time to daily study. *Torah*, they believed, was

like a slice of bread eaten every day, and without it, Jews had no appetite for life. Crafts and trade were just for reaching the main target in life – studying Torah, because only through Torah does man merit eternity.

Shabbes, the weekly day of rest, offered a taste of that world to come, when prayer and spirituality replaced daily cares. Pinczow's two-storey stone synagogue, one of the oldest in Poland, was famed for its numerous *Torah* scrolls, embroidered curtains, beautiful murals and distinctive architectural style.

By the 1795 Polish Partition, some of Pinczow's Jews, clothed in traditional long dark coats, worked as shopkeepers, furriers, shoemakers, traders and exporters. Others served the community as matchmakers, circumcisers, butchers and bakers. Because the *Torah* forbids wearing woollen fabric interwoven with linen, however, fully half laboured as weavers, tailors and hatters. They clothed Jew and Gentile alike.

In 1815, Pinczow, incorporated into Congress Poland, came under harsh, anti-Semitic Russian rule. A decade later, Tsar Nicholas I, determined to integrate Jews into Russian society, enacted hundreds of anti-Semitic laws. In addition to initiating compulsory Jewish military service, he also abolished autonomous Jewish communities, curtailed the publication of Jewish books, established Jewish government schools that taught secular subjects and forbade traditional Jewish garb and side-locks. Pinczow's Jews, increasingly taxed, could barely make a living.

According to an anonymous nobleman,

Surely there is no [more] wretched race under the sun [than] the poor Jewish people who dwell in ... Pinczow ... . With the minor exception of a few with greater means, there dwell in one small room which is stricken with a plague-ridden miasma, over a dozen Jews, begrimed, halfnaked [sic], who lie down at night in actual layers one over the other in hammocks, engaged in an almost incessant struggle with hunger, illness, and all too often even with death, without help or hope in this world, save for the courage imbedded in the heart by reason of strong faith despite all the many afflictions which bedevil them. There is indeed no uglier sight than these towns ridden by this plague; nothing touches one's heart more than the poverty of this people over whom the curse holds unrestrained sway in a manner so plainly visible. Observing the multitude of gloomy faces of Jewry wending its plodding way in our towns, the thoughtful person will ask, perforce, on what does this poor people sustain its life?

Jewish conscription reached Pinczow in 1834. In addition to adults, youngsters, some as young as 5 years old, were spirited into pre-army cantonist schools. All, from age 18, served on active duty for twenty years, followed by an additional five years in the reserves.

Military conscription weighed heavily on all Jewish communities. Military service not only contradicted their basic reverence for life, but also distanced Jews from religious practice, *kosher* food and scholarship. Many recruits, ill-treated and intensely pressured to convert, Heaven forefend, forsook their faith altogether. Rather than lose their sons forever, rather than lose their souls as well, Jewish parents often bribed officials to falsify birth records or hired peasants to take their place. When these measures failed, many often urged their youngsters to flee the country. Ze'ev Wolf, an only son, left Pinczow in 1846, accompanied by his older sister, Eva. He was nearly 12 years old.

According to family lore, the pair headed north by horse-drawn cart across Prussia. Although no record of their journey has been found, they may have boarded a new-fangled steamship at Danzig, a major Baltic port over 250 miles away.

Nothing is known of their background, but the name of their father, who appears in an early source as Dovid Yehuda HaLevi. Although traditional son-of names were required in Jewish ritual, it became increasingly difficult as Europe's *Ashkenazi* population grew to differentiate between the many Dovids, son of Yehuda Leibs, and Yehuda Leibs, son of Dovids. With Jewish names so common, so confusing, how could the Russian Empire effect all-inclusive taxation and conscription?

Though names posed the problem, names also provided the solution. In the late 1700s, Russian Jews were assigned or ordered to adopt surnames that would conclusively differentiate one from another. Families often chose surnames derived from their places of origin, personal characteristics or occupations. Others, like Dovid Yehuda Leib, retained their religious honorifics, like HaLevi or HaCohen.

The Children of Israel, as they fled ancient Egypt, were divided into three groups, Israelites, Levites and Cohens. Cohens, direct descendants of Aaron the Priest, and Levites, members of the tribe of Levi, were charged with important religious obligations. Although these dwindled after the destruction of Jerusalem's Holy Temple, their titles, like those of nobility, continued to pass down orally from father to son. No wonder Ze'ev, though anglicizing his father's name in British documents, retained the name Levi.

Ze'ev does not appear in England's 1851 census. Yet, reveals *The Jewish Chronicle*, a year later, one Woolf Davis, a name by which he was later known, donated funds to the Society For Supporting Fanny's Orphans. His address, also noted, was 109 Gravel Lane, Houndsditch, City of London.

Neither does Woolf Davis appear in the 1851 census. Yet two rag merchants, John and Isaac Levy, also living at 109 Gravel Lane, do. Could Ze'ev Yitzhak Dovid HaLevi, aka Woolf Davis, have gone under a third name too?

Possibly. New immigrants, though they could alter neither their telltale accents nor their foreign demeanour, often tried to assimilate by changing their names. Journalist Charles Manby Smith observed, tongue in cheek, that 'dealing with Jews has induced many of them to disguise or change their names. Thus Moses sometimes becomes Moss, Abraham sinks into Braham, or expands into Tabraham, and Levi is anagramed into Evil, &c.'

Though far-fetched, perhaps Ze'ev Yitzhak Dovid HaLevi omitted his and his father's first names, leaving Yitzchak Halevi. Then, by translating Yitzhak (Hebrew) to Isaac, and shortening HaLevi, he became a dapper-sounding Isaac Levy. Perhaps he arrived at Woolf Davis by translating Ze'ev (wolf in Hebrew) to a more distinguished spelling, then anglicizing David (Dovid in Yiddish) to Davis.

By 1851, Woolf's sister Eva was married and living at Mansell Street, City of London, an area of importers, wholesalers and cigar, pencil and sealing-wax manufacturers. She and her brother, like their father before them, likely cut brims and crowns from worn skirts and coats, stitching them into caps. Because Britain's working classes caps slouched rakishly to one side and upper classes sported them for casual pursuits, cloth caps commanded quite a market. In fact, relates Bill Williams,

Cap making was the boom industry of the late 1840s and 50s. The first

in the field as entrepreneurs … rose rapidly on the economic scale …
Successful retailers in other lines … switched direction to cap making
on the basis of immigrant labour. More resilient paupers … found in
cap making the means to substantial independence.

In 1852, Woolf Davis, living at 109 Gravel Lane, wed Sarah Rachel
Magnus, a Polish immigrant who lived on Mansell Street, near his sister Eva.
   Their first child, name unknown, was apparently born at Royal Mint
Street, Aldgate. By the time Maurice, their second, arrived in 1855, the family
had moved to narrow New Castle (today Tyne) Street, Whitechapel, a
crowded area known for its lack of sanitation and poverty. Woolf, like his
tailor and dressmaker neighbours, probably laboured at home, amid mounds
of highly flammable cloth.
   Within two years, the family moved to Church (today Fournier) Street,
Spitalfields, a 'residence of choice for successful business families in the area'.
As Sarah neared the end of her next pregnancy, Woolf purchased Sun
Insurance fire coverage for his New Castle property, which he probably
retained as his workshop. Abraham Davis was born six days later.
   Their next son, Isidore, arrived in 1858, followed by Jacob, in 1859. That
same year, in a step unusual for Jews at the time, Woolf received British
naturalization. Since applications were reviewed by the police and required
personal character references, citizenship increased his personal and
professional standing considerably. Besides, it proved that he was fluent in
English.
   Sarah and Woolf then welcomed six more boys, Hyman (1860), David
(1862), Joseph (1864), Nathan (1868), Ralph (1871) and Harry (1873). All
were born in Spitalfields.
   Because Woolf remained observant, he probably provided his sons with
religious, as well as secular, educations. His four youngest attended London's

Woolf Davis, living at 109 Gravel Lane, married Sarah Rachel Magnus in 1852. *Lois Kaufman*

Jews' Free School. His older sons may have as well; ledgers for the relevant years are not available.

Life in Spitalfields was not easy. This market district, which had long welcomed East European Jewish immigrants, now swelled with Irish newcomers fleeing the Great Potato Famine. Its streets and alleyways, where two to three families often shared common housing, were cramped and congested. Evictions, due to the uncertainty of employment compounded by high rents, was common. Prostitution was rife, along with beggary, thievery and drunkenness. Mortality was high due to an array of communicable diseases and poor sanitation, which, in 1866, ushered in a cholera epidemic.

While many Jews worked as independent craftsmen or laboured in small factories and workshops, others lived by marginal means. Some ran saloons, gambling dens or brothels. Others confined debtors to sponging houses or peddled their wares in barrows and stalls on the street.

Henry Mayhew, a social researcher and journalist, observed that

A commercial traveller told me he could never leave town by any 'mail' or 'stage', without being besieged by a small army of Jewish boys, who most pertinaciously offered him oranges, lemons, sponges, combs, pocket-books, pencils, sealing-wax, paper, many-bladed pen-knives, razors, pocket-mirrors, and shaving boxes – as if a man could not possibly quit the metropolis without requiring a stock of those commodities.

Over time, however, fewer and fewer Jews became hawkers. Since hawking courted abuse, it was often hazardous. Besides, because the Irish could live harder, they undersold their Jewish neighbours. Hawking had become less profitable.

So Jewish street-sellers, rather than grooming their sons to follow their example, directed them toward community-sponsored apprenticeships or semi-skilled labour in workshops. Many second-generation immigrants crafted and marketed the very items that their grandfathers had once peddled, like lead pencils, sealing-wax, looking-glasses, umbrellas and brushes.

For others, observes Todd M. Endelman, commerce,

became the vehicle for the economic transformation of Anglo-Jewry … . native-born middle ranks of English Jewry were filled with the children and grandchildren of peddlers, old clothes men, and market traders who had become respectable, if modest, businessmen. A striking illustration of this can be seen in the … orange trade. [Significantly,] by mid-century, Jews were no longer the dominant group hawking oranges in the streets of London, having been replaced by the Irish. However, they remained prominent at the wholesale end of the trade: the fruit market in Duke's Place, where street traders purchased oranges and nuts, was entirely Jewish. A similar development occurred in the secondhand clothing trade. Jews increasingly moved out of the lower end of the trade and into its slightly more salubrious branches, becoming pawnbrokers, slopsellers, auctioneers, salesmen with fixed premises, or stallholders …

Others, like frame makers, watchmakers and quill makers, transformed their expertise and experience into specialty antique, jewellery, or stationery businesses.

After Eva, Woolf's widowed sister, died following a long illness in 1879, he supported her children, several of whom were described as 'deaf and dumb'. Moreover, he provided for them in his will.

By 1881, when floods of Jewish Polish-Russian refugees were crowding the East End, Woolf had become a master furrier. He found a ready-made market.

During the winter, Victorians typically bundled up in fashionable fur-tipped tippets, boas, capes, great coats, jackets, scarves, cloaks, shawls, thick socks, stockings, long wraps, caps, hats and ear muffs when venturing outdoors. Those travelling in open sleighs, carts and carriages also snuggled under fur-lined comforters, rugs, quilts or blankets. Sealskin coats prevented wind and rain from penetrating to the skin and swansdown muffs kept delicate hands snug and protected.

Furriers' work conditions, reveals novelist Israel Zangwill, were horrendous.

> … over everything was the trail of the fur. The air was full of a fine fluff – a million little hairs floated about the room covering everything, insinuating themselves everywhere, getting down the backs of the workers and tickling them, getting into their lungs and making them cough, getting into their food and drink and sickening them … . They awoke with 'furred' tongues, and they went to bed with them. The irritating filaments gathered on their clothes, on their faces, on the crockery, on the sofa, on the mirrors … an impalpable down overlaying everything, penetrating even to the drinking-water in the board-covered zinc bucket … . And in this room they sat – man, woman, boy – bending over boas bewitching young ladies would skate in; stitch, stitch … winter and summer …

Since Woolf's fur business does not appear in local retail trade directories, he may actually have dealt in, rather than processed, furs. If so, it proved lucrative. Within a short while, he was able to dabble in real estate, purchasing, brokering, and letting properties, probably as investments.

Soon Maurice and Abraham Davis, inspired by their father's success, also began negotiating property investments and brokerage. Though they apparently had received no formal training in any building art, they, singly and in pairs, began constructing edifices of their own. Isobel Watson explains why the time was ripe.

> Much of the physical manifestation of London's rapid expansion in the early nineteenth century took the form of two-storey speculatively-built and badly-drained terraced dwellings, often in the over-built rear courtyards of deteriorating property … . Those who suffered were not only the very poor, but also artisans, clerks and a wide sector in stable wage-earning employment who aspired to cleanliness and respectability. … the main force in the generation and regeneration of the urban fabric remained the speculative builder … . largely unregulated, save by rudimentary sanitary and structural requirements …

By the 1880s, the Davis family left increasingly crowded Spitalfields for Navarino Villas in Dalston, a middle class East London suburb popular among prosperous Jewish tradesmen. During the next twenty years, they moved to more and more prestigious areas of London – Highbury New Park, West Hampstead, then Goldhurst Terrace. It was here that Sarah died in 1900.

The following year, Woolf and his sons donated 'two very handsome' floral stained-glass windows in her memory, to the Dennington Park Road Hampstead Synagogue, where he was an active member.

Three years later, Woolf married Louisa (Lucy) Cohen, a 62-year-old spinster, beneath those very windows. When she died a decade later, she, like Sarah, was laid to rest in the Davis family plot at the Willesden Cemetery, London. Woolf, who repaired to a more modest, ten-room dwelling at Inglewood Road, West Hampstead after her death, died in 1917. He rests near both his wives.

In his will, Woolf left two oil portraits of his first wife's parents (which have since disappeared) to his sons. He also left them all his monetary possessions on one condition – that they remain Jewish. His greatest legacy, however, was his sons themselves, men of initiative, business acumen, daring, vision and a moral compass tempered by Jewish values.

Woolf Davis with sons Maurice and Abraham. *Lois Kaufman*

Abraham Davis and family, 1895. *Lois Kaufman*

Over a span of thirty-some years, six of them, Maurice, Abraham, Isidore, Hyman, Nathan and Ralph, individually and in partnership, built varied, imaginative projects throughout London. Whenever any encountered financial crises or other difficulties along the way, they relied on each other for advice and financial support.

Hyman and Isidore, working as a team, built flats, as well as freehold and leasehold commercial properties, throughout London's East End. Some of their edifices still stand today.

After Hyman's death in 1902, Isidore and his wife Minnie founded the Davis cinema circuit at Highgate. Until then, reveals Isidore's son Alfred, 'films had been exhibited in crudely converted music halls and shops'. It is claimed that the Electric Pavilion at Highgate [one of his father's projects] was "the first cinema absolutely built for cinema work in London"'. Cinemas in Shepherds Bush, Marble Arch, Croydon and elsewhere followed. The Ritzy Brixton, formerly the Electric Pavilion, still delights crowds today.

Nathan and Ralph Davis erected blocks of red brick flats together. Maurice built flats, carved brickwork buildings framed by characteristic ornamental iron fences, and 'crow-stepped gabled shops' throughout the East End. He also introduced a mix of small flats and workshops that appealed to the Jewish community.

Abraham, the most prolific Davis brother, rebuilt scores of flats and tenement blocks across London's East End, as well as mansions in St Pancras and huge, post-1900 'service' blocks in St John's Wood. By designing and raising thousands more, he also transformed slums into pleasant living areas. Both in partnership and on his own, Abraham also constructed warehouses, a Jewish food market and the Moorish Market, an innovative, covered shopping centre boasting sixty-three shops, in Fashion Street, Spitalfields. Its façade still exists today.

Abraham named several buildings for his wife Helena and several blocks for his children, Irene, Ruth, Josephine, Winfred and Godfrey. He also named large projects, like the Davis Mansions, after his family.

Abraham installed innovative lifts in a number of his blocks, patenting a related system that delivered meals to private flats from a central kitchen. He established the London Housing Society to provide homes for the working class, and pioneered public and private housing financed through post-First World War government subsidies. He also built self-contained flats for professional single women on annual tenancies.

Clearly, Abraham was as concerned with London's social needs as much as his personal commercial success. Yet in September 1902, during the

Abraham Davis built huge, post-1900 'service' blocks. *Isobel Watson*

unpleasant period just before the establishment of the Royal Commission on Alien Immigration which resulted in the 1905 Aliens Act, an anonymous reader wrote the editor of the *East London Observer*:

> Passing along Batty Street, Commercial-road, and looking at a block of buildings in course of erection by Messrs Davis Brothers for Jewish tenants, my eye caught a motto on the front of the building, viz. 'Work, wait, win', which means the Jewish community will capture London, and eventually England, without firing a shot.

With thanks to Lois Kaufman, great-great-grand-daughter of Woolf and Sarah Rachel Davis.

Documents

Vital records

Abraham Davis, birth record, in *Birth Records of the Great & Hambro Synagogue,* Harold and Miriam Lewin, London: privately published, 2008.

Woolf Davis-Louisa Cohen, July-August-September 1903, 1a/1597, *England and Wales Civil Registration Indexes,* GRO.

Woolf Davis-Rachel Magnus, marriage contract, 8 December 1852, London Great Synagogue, in *Marriage Records of the Great Synagogue, London, 1791-1885,* Harold and Miriam Lewin, Jerusalem: privately printed, 2004.

DISCOVER MORE ABOUT HISTORY

Wharncliffe Books are an imprint of Pen & Sword Books who now have over 2000 titles in print covering all aspects of history. Wharncliffe specialise in local history and have a number of leading titles in print. 2008 has seen the launch of two new imprints in the Wharncliffe name, True Crime and Transport. These books will cover all aspects of crime and transport, both on a local and national scale. If you would like to receive more information and special offers on your preferred interests along with our standard catalogue, please complete and return this card (no stamp required in the UK). Alternatively, register online at www.pen-and-sword.co.uk. Thank you. **PLEASE NOTE: We do not sell data information to any third party companies.**

Mr/Mrs/Ms/Other.............Name...............

Address.................

..................Postcode............

Email address...........

LOCAL HISTORY		TRANSPORT		TRUE CRIME	
Guides	☐	Railways	☐	Foul Deeds	☐
Industrial History	☐	Cars	☐	Conmen/Hoaxes	☐
Family History	☐	Buses/Trams	☐	Serial Killers	☐
Nostalgia	☐	Canals	☐	ALL THE ABOVE	☐

Website: www.pen-and-sword.co.uk • Email: enquiries@pen-and-sword.co.uk
Telephone: 01226 734555 • Fax: 01226 734438

Wharncliffe Books
FREEPOST SF5
47 Church Street
BARNSLEY
South Yorkshire
S70 2BR

2

Census Records
Isaac Levy [John Levy] household, HO107, 1524/223, TNA.
Joseph Solomons household. HO107, 1546/7, TNA.
Jacob [sic] Solomons household, RG9, 273/54, TNA.
Woolf Davis household, RG10, 503/27, TNA.
Woolf Davis household, RG11, 435/4, TNA.
Woolf Davis household, RG12, 173/105, TNA.
Woolf Davis household, RG13, 330/124, TNA.
Woolf Davis household, RG14, 640/unspecified, TNA.

Other
Anonymous letter, *The East London Observer*, 13 September 1902, microfilm, Tower Hamlets Local History Library & Archives.
Email, 20 July 2010, Lois Kaufman to author, referencing Alfred Davis.
Jews' Free School Admission and Discharge Registers, Boys, 1869–1939, 4046/C/01/ 1, LMA.
Sun Insurance Policy 1823276, 12 March 1857, Guildhall Library MS 11936, LMA.
Will, Woolf Davis, 14 March 1916. PRO, TNA.
Woolf Davis, Naturalization Record, PRO, HO 1/88/2831, TNA

Bibliography
Alderman, Geoffrey, *Modern British Jewry*, Oxford: Clarendon Press, New York, Oxford University Press, 1992.
Ehrenbourg, Ilya, 'Reb Yosele and the Brazlav Hasidin', *Jewish Caravan*, Leo W. Schwarz, editor, New York: Farrar & Rinehart, 1935, 373–77.
Ellis, Robert (F.L.S.), Great Britain. Commissioners for the Exhibition of 1851, *Official Descriptive and Illustrated Catalogue*, vol. 2, London: Spicer Brothers, 1851. http://books.google.com Retrieved 22 July 2010.
Endelman, Todd M., *The Jews of Britain, 1656 to 2000*, Berkeley, CA: University of California Press, 2002.
Grossbaum-Pasternak, Rachel, 'Pinzcow', Hebrew, Jerry Tepperman, translator, *Pinkas HaKehillot, Polen*, vol. VII, Jerusalem: Yad VaShem, 1999: 392–6, *Kielce-Radom SIG Journal* vol. 5, no. 1, Winter 2001: 3. www.jewishgen.org Retrieved 22 April 2012.
'Hampstead Synagogue', 6 December 1901, *The Jewish Chronicle*: 30.
Mahler, Raphael, Eugene Orenstein, Jenny Machlowitz Klein, translators, *Hasidism and the Jewish Enlightenment: Their Confrontation in Galicia and Poland in the First Half of the Nineteenth Century*, Philadelphia: Jewish Publication Society, 1985.
Mayhew, Henry, *London Labour and the London Poor*, vol. II, London: Charles Griffin and Company, Exeter Street, Strand, 1851. http://books.google.com http://books.google.com Retrieved 31 May 2010.
Sanborn, Vic. 'Keeping Warm in the Regency Era, Part One'. http://janeaustensworld. wordpress.com Retrieved 26 August, 2010.
Shemer, M., editor, *Sefer Zikaron le-Kehilat Pintshev*, Hebrew, translated by the author, Tel Aviv: Former Residents of Pinczow in Israel and the Diaspora, 1970.
Smith, Charles Manby, 'Genesis of the Workers', *The Little World of London*, London: Arthur Hall, Virtue and Co., 25, Paternoster Row, 1857, *The Victorian Dictionary*, Lee Jackson, compiler. http://www.victorianlondon.org

'Society For Supporting Fanny's Orphans', *The Jewish Chronicle*, 5 November 1852: 32.

'Society For Supporting Fanny's Orphans', *The Jewish Chronicle*, 19 November 1852:48.

Watson, Isobel, *'Rebuilding London: Abraham Davis and his Brothers, 1881–1924'*, *London Journal* 29 (1), 2004.

Williams, Bill, *The Making of Manchester Jewry* 1740–1875, Manchester: Manchester University Press, 1985.

Zangwill, Israel, *The King of Schnorrers: Grotesques and Fantasies*, Chestnut Hill, Massachusetts: Elibron Classics, 2006. http://books.google.comhttp://books.google.com http://books.google.com Retrieved 16 August 2010.

Chapter 4

Samuel Wolfsohn

Posen Province, Prussian-Poland to Sheffield, 1857

'… when constabulary duty's to be done…
A policeman's lot is not a happy one …'
Pirates of Penzance, Gilbert & Sullivan.

Little is known of Samuel Wolfsohn's origins. By 1861, however, the 29-year-old was lodging with the Williams family, their servant, and a visiting Jewish family, at Melinda Terrace, Sheffield, South Yorkshire, possibly sharing a clay-brick cottage tiled with local slate. If so, Wolfsohn, who was single, may have slept beneath the eaves above a room that served as kitchen, scullery, dining area and bathroom.

The young man was evidently active in the local Jewish community, since he witnessed the 'Albu Affair', an internal row that split Sheffield's Figtree Lane Synagogue to its roots.

Several wealthy congregants, after the completion of Figtree Lane renovations, had publicly ousted Isaac Guttman, a donor who had fallen into arrears in his dues, from the festive re-consecration ceremony. Guttman's brother, while protesting this familial slight, goaded a fellow member, Ephraim Jacobs, into physically attacking him.

Reverend Berthold Albu, the synagogue's cantor-circumciser and ritual slaughterer, attempted to restore peace between the two, but to no avail. Instead, Jacobs formally charged Guttman with brawling. When Guttman subpoenaed Albu as a court witness in his defence, for some reason, the learned man, though he had seen the fight unfold, failed to support his account. Because this raised doubts about Albu's personal integrity, he was charged with perjury. On the strength of this alone, he was summarily dismissed from his position.

Although the perjury charges against Albu were eventually withdrawn, his dismissal remained final. In response to an advertisement seeking his replacement, twelve registered synagogue members and nine permanent seat-holders, including Samuel Wolfsohn, penned a petition to *The Jewish Chronicle*, expressing their desire that he remain at his post.

Meriting a permanent synagogue seat, which bespeaks presence and power, suggests that Samuel or his family had joined the Sheffield Jewish community years earlier. Two family heirlooms, Hebrew-English High Holiday Day prayer books printed in 1799 London, seem to support this conjecture. Yet no record of previous Wolfsohns in Sheffield has yet been found.

Enterprising peddlers, who made, repaired, and sold low-cost umbrellas, brushes, used clothing, or trinkets, were probably the first Jews to seek economic opportunity outside London. As they ventured farther and farther afoot however, they also distanced themselves from religious necessities like *kosher* food and prayer quorums. Soon networks of Jewish-run lodging houses sprang up in their wake, allowing them to stay afield for longer periods. Where traders found their religious and economic needs met, their families often followed.

The first Jews, who reached Sheffield in 1786, were apparently an engraver, a victualler and a merchant. Jewish silversmiths, pawnbrokers, tailors, tobacconists, cobblers, dentists, cart-owners, potters, drapers, spring knife manufacturers and cutlers, attracted by the town's growing economic opportunities, soon followed. Initially, they held prayers in private homes, employing locals as cantors and ritual slaughterers.

In time, a small number respected for their business acumen, were elected to local civic office. Not all served, however. Maurice Bright, for example, was barred from Sheffield's Town Council for refusing to swear the mandatory Christian oath of acceptance. Yet this did not hinder his appointment, in 1827, as the local Police Commissioner.

Sheffield's fledgling Jewish community leased two small cemeteries, a sure sign of permanent settlement, in 1831. Yet they acquired their permanent Figtree Lane synagogue building only a decade later.

In 1852, writes Neville David Ballin, the synagogue paid its cantor-ritual slaughterer twenty-four shillings a week

A house was provided, rent and rates free, and two loads of coal per annum were included. His duties stipulated that he must kill twice a week at two butchers, kill poultry at home when required, and attend each butcher's shop one hour per morning and not accept any gifts. He also had to teach three times a week … . The children paid him one penny … for the lessons …' [likely in the basics of Judaism – Hebrew, then Torah.]

In the 1861 census, Wolfsohn, like many Sheffield Jewish immigrants, reveals his birthplace as 'Poland, Not Known'. Borders, during his lifetime, were indeed confusing. After Napoleon's defeat at Waterloo in 1815, Austria, Prussia and the Russian Empire carved up the Duchy of Warsaw, which had encompassed much of historic Poland, among themselves. Other areas, incorporated into Congress Poland, fell under Russian rule. Although the official State of Poland had ceased to exist, Yiddish-speaking Samuel, because he hailed from a Polish-speaking area, considered himself a Pole.

Samuel was possibly Sheffield's first Jewish constable. For decades past, aside from an occasional Irish or Scotsman, all Sheffield's policemen had been locally born and bred. Since English literacy was a firm requirement for acceptance to the force, Samuel had either arrived at a very early age or possessed a fine ear for languages. He may have boasted another trait that enforcers of the law often lacked at the time, sobriety.

During the nineteenth century, Sheffield, one of Britain's largest towns, became renowned for its innovative methods of steel production, especially Sheffield plate, which features silver and copper layers in a wide range of household items. As the city's economy prospered, its population grew remarkably fast. With little provision for expansion, however, its citizens, crowded together, endured robberies, violence and murder. Moreover, reported *The New York Times* in 1867, the harsh nature of Sheffield's cutlery industry also bred crime.

> Where people are accustomed to accidents with powder, to accidents by the splitting and flying of grinding wheels, and to accidents by the misuse of edge tools, it is not unnatural that they should get to regard acts of violence with a certain degree of indifference … . A man who is every moment in danger of losing his eyes or his fingers by an instant's carelessness or bad luck, and who expects to have his lungs worn into holes by steel filings before he is forty years of age, is naturally disposed to be violent and careless about both life and limb. … The high price of manual skill of course makes those who possess it passionately desirous to retain their advantages, and [i]ntensely jealous of every contrivance which can possibly reduce their importance. These circumstances undoubtedly go a long way to explain the fact of the bad eminence of Sheffield over other places …

Sheffield did indeed suffer several serious labour conflicts. Within a month, 'After meeting to devise measures for continuing their strike,' wrote *The New York Times*, 'a number of men who had been "locked-out", attacked the houses of some non-unionists and sacked them. A great riot followed, but it was finally stopped by the Police, who succeeded in dispersing the mob.'

In addition to fighting crime, Sheffield's police dealt with emergencies and natural disasters. Samuel Harrison, a local journalist, reported that during the Great Sheffield Flood of 1864, which devastated large areas of town, killing hundreds,

> The exertions of the police in connection with the flood were most arduous and praiseworthy ... . The labours which the flood threw upon the police were very heavy, and all the members of the force deserve praise for their great and successful exertions.

With all this responsibility, all this danger, why would anyone want to become a policeman? Had they not, most candidates, who were largely unskilled, would have faced a lifetime of drudgery in a colliery, field or a factory. But why might Samuel have chosen police work over traditional Jewish trades and crafts? Perhaps he had firm friends among the force. Perhaps he preferred an outdoor rough and tumble life to one of less adventurous pawnbroking, tailoring, or cobbling. Or perhaps he valued law enforcement for its job security, respectability, opportunity for advancement, and no less important, its warm uniforms.

A policeman's lot, however, like that of most labourers, was not easy. Leaves were few, with no regard for Sabbaths, Sundays, or public holidays. Pay, though steady, was poor, and discipline strict. Low-ranking constables were frequently fined for breaking wind whilst on parade, for associating with known prostitutes, or for gossiping on duty. Samuel himself was once fined a shilling for appearing with a dirty 'bull's eye' lantern and a sixpence for turning up late on parade.

Despite these minor lapses, Wolfsohn made a name for himself, sometimes in unexpected ways. According to family lore, he enjoyed having fellow police officers over for congenial evenings of sniffing snuff, and he once caught a burglar making his escape over Sheffield's rooftops by biting him on the hand, thereby earning a ceremonial baton. Moreover, in 1861, he seized a mugger upon overhearing him threaten a maiden with a line lifted from an old Sheffield ballad, 'Money I want and money I'll have!'

Samuel married Jeanette Basch later that year. Although no photographs of their wedding have survived (if ever there were any), Wolfsohn, if he fulfilled police requirements, stood at least 175cm (5ft 8.5in) tall. He may have also boasted a long, luxurious, double-pointed beard, which was very fashionable at the time.

Jacob Basch, 29, and his 'daughter', 19. *Census Returns of England and Wales* 1861.

Jeanette's physical attributes remain a mystery. So do her origins. Though the 1861 census indicates that she, at 19, was the daughter of 29-year-old Jacob Basch, their ages do not add up. Both Jacob and Jeanette, however, in their marriage contract, note that their father was 'Isaac Basch, cap maker'. Moreover, both named their firstborn sons 'Isaac', possibly following the Jewish tradition of memorializing deceased loved ones. So the two may have actually been siblings.

The census enumerator, however, noted that Jacob was born in Sheffield and Jeanette in Prussia. This seems to be in error. Because the earliest known documentation of a Basch in Sheffield, and indeed in all England, is Jacob's 1855 marriage contract, Prussia became the springboard for further research.

Investigation has revealed that an Isaac Basch, a cap maker born in 1801 in Graetz, Posen Province, Prussia (today Grodzisk Wielkopolski, Poland), had a son named Jacob. Since Isaac Basch of Graetz named his son Jacob and Jacob Basch of Sheffield named his son Isaac, the two, based on the interchange of given names, may have been related. Yet who can say for sure? Steven Frais, a great-great-grandson of Jacob Basch of Sheffield shares his doubts.

Although I know from English records that I am descended from a Prussian cap manufacturer called Isaac BASCH who had a son called Jacob, and there was such a person in Graetz and the dates fit, I don't see how I could possibly be sure that this is my ancestor and not just someone who happens to have the same name and occupation. Both Isaac and Jacob are common forenames. On the other hand, perhaps the BASCH family of Graetz and my ancestors are one and the same. If this is so, I feel that Samuel Wolfsohn came from the Posen area – like the Baschs – and hence the match.

Although Jews did often marry into families from their places of origin, this initially was conjecture. Yet when Frais discovered an entry that, by inference, placed a Wolf Samuel Wolfsohn, born c1790, in tiny Neustadt bei Pinne, scarcely ten miles away, his assumption gained credibility.

Wolf Wolfsohn's middle name, however, is confusing. When Napoleon ordered Jews to adopt surnames in 1808, did the youthful Wolf, in addition to adopting the surname Wolf-sohn, also retain the name of his father, Samuel? Possibly. In Judaism, a father's given name identifies a man for the length of his life. Yet even if Wolfsohn (son-of Samuel, deceased) did name *his* son Samuel after his father, as Jews often do, the question remains. Were Samuel Wolfsohn of Sheffield and Wolf Samuel Wolfsohn of Neustadt bei Pinne, though separated by time and space, actually related?

Although it is unclear when Jews first arrived in Neustadt bei Pinne (today Lwowek, Poland), the community was well established by 1725. That year its Lord of the Manor granted his Jews a 'privilegium', laying down a multitude of official laws, fines and duties. Along with guarantee of community electoral autonomy, he allowed them to swear oaths according to their custom, employ a rabbi, work as tailors, trade in 'iron, cloth, rope, leather, lace, silk ribbons and bows' (but not salt and herring), and receive free wood to build their homes. In return, they were to serve on the town watch, pay 'Jewish' taxes (with no exemptions), and 'supply the castle with meat against payment' – but save the hearts of the slaughtered animals for the birds. Since fires were commonplace, Jewish landlords, and likely all property owners, were also required to own fire hoses and water tubs. After a huge blaze swept through Neustadt in 1813, destroying the synagogue and many homes, scores of Jews resettled in other villages across Posen Province.

In 1833, Posen's Jews received the right to establish religious associations. Since most continued to suffer deep poverty, their children were also required, by law, to learn trades. Yet economic and political discrimination continued. Jewish men, for example, could marry only after age 24, after proving that they could support their families. Because naturalized Jews were allowed to leave Posen Province, however, many sought opportunity elsewhere.

Despite this, the Neustadt Jewish community, by 1840, boasted over 800 Jewish souls, a third of its entire population. Five years later, disaster struck. Raging floods, precipitated by vast amounts of thawing ice and snow, destroyed local harvests. The resulting poverty and starvation triggered cholera and typhoid epidemics.

By 1846, observes Ismar Elbogen, Posen Jews suffered politically as well.

> ... the government had wished to place petty restrictions upon the rights of all Jews and to set special disabilities upon the Jews of Posen, who constituted 40% of all the Jews of Prussia ... . The memorandum which the government submitted came to the remarkable conclusion that Jews were wanting in sense of honour, in gentleness, and in the philanthropic impulse, and sought to explain this condition by reference to the Jews' business activities, their poverty, and their lack of schooling.

During the 1848 Spring of Nations revolution, one of many political upheavals sweeping Europe that year, the Jews of Posen Province maintained neutrality. Their Christian neighbours, who had courted them with jobs and additional rights in return for support during uprisings, however, reacted with violence. Perhaps this, combined with growing economic pressure, encouraged increasing numbers of Posen's Jews to leave for elsewhere.

Some settled in Berlin. Others crossed Prussia on foot, by cart, or by rail toward ports along the North Sea. Ship records reveal that a Basch, first name unknown, reached Britain from Ostend, Belgium in 1849, possibly aboard a propeller-driven steamer. Eight years later, an S. Wolfson [sic] followed in his footsteps. These were not necessarily Jacob Basch and Samuel Wolfsohn of Sheffield, of course. Yet, for the meantime, these are the only known records with any relevance.

In any case, by the time they reached Sheffield, a Polish-Jewish hawker, silversmith, grocer, and Hebrew and German teacher, along with a handful of accountants, jewellers, pawnbrokers and tailors, had also joined its Jewish community.

When the Wolfsohn's first child, Isaac, arrived in 1862, the family was living in Dun Fields, Sheffield, an extremely crowded labourers' area. Most of their neighbours – rollers, file cutters and cutlers – worked in the local steel industry.

While Samuel kept law and order, Basch, his brother-in-law, fashioned cloth caps, an almost exclusively Jewish trade. Like most in the clothing

S. Wolfson, arrival record, Ostende, Belgium, 1857. *England, Alien Arrivals*

industry, he probably laboured in cramped, unsanitary 'sweat' conditions for up to fourteen hours a day, for pay that dwindled to nearly nothing during slow seasons. Over time, Basch's financial situation, poor to begin with, deteriorated even further. Finally, in 1869, the 'Cap manufacturer and Dealer', adjudged bankrupt, was ordered to 'surrender himself' to Registrars of the County Court for a hearing.

In a short while, Basch and his family left Sheffield for Manchester, some fifty miles away along the Manchester, Sheffield and Lincolnshire Railway Line. Since this large, industrial centre boasted a flourishing economy, he surely expected to find a high demand for cloth caps. The Wolfsohns, evidently very close to the couple, followed soon after.

Liverpool-based, Jewish-German traders first reached Manchester in the late 1700s. At the turn of the century, Nathan Meyer, a founder of the Rothschild Dynasty, joined them, establishing thriving textile and financial businesses, before settling in London.

As early as 1804, the Manchester Jewish community, which initially conducted prayers in a local warehouse, offered wintertime relief, probably food and coal, to the needy. Over the years, its growth, fuelled by recurring religious schisms, led to the establishment of additional houses of worship including the orthodox Great Synagogue, and a reform synagogue, one of the first in Britain.

Scores of Jewish immigrants, fleeing poverty and persecution, passed through Manchester after the inauguration of the Manchester Victoria Railway Station in 1844. A vast number were transmigrants.

When shipping and British railroad companies linked up services, masses of emigrants disembarked at east coast British ports like Hull, Grimsby, London, or Leith, then seamlessly took cheap, fast trains to west coast ports. There they boarded great trans-Atlantic steamships bound for America, Canada, or farther.

A far smaller number of arrivals, travel-weary, rendered penniless, or sensing economic opportunity, paused or stayed in Leeds, Glasgow, Liverpool and London's East End. Many, like the Basch and Wolfsohn families, also settled in Manchester's crowded Red Bank district.

As Isaac Franklin noted in 1870, the area was notorious for its

> close, dirty, ill-ventilated and ill-drained habitations ... [that encouraged] high infant mortality and rapid spread of infectious diseases. ... Most of the streets were unlit. ... The drains were choked by the lie of the land, the wells tainted, the air polluted by the 'pestilential effluvia' of the Irk – that 'turbid river, loaded with the refuse of every kind of manufacture and decomposing matter' ...

Yet Red Bank's streets, which resounded with Yiddish, also offered easy access to *cheders, kosher* butchers and ritual baths. Its *chevros,* a network of warm, intimate prayer groups similar to the *shtieblich* of their home towns, offered newcomers from Cracow, Warsaw or Kovno, for example, the warm, familiar *Yiddishkeit* of East European ghetto life.

Worshippers, observed Israel Zangwill, came

> two and three times a day to batter the gates of heaven and to listen to sermons more exegetical than ethical. They dropped in, mostly in their workaday garments and grime, and rumbled and roared and chorused prayers with a zeal that shook the windowpanes, and there was never a lack of a minyan – the congregational quorum of ten.

Chevros often doubled as club houses as well, with members proffering advice, material support, and care for the needy. Some even offered lodging.

Manchester's Anglo-Jewish establishment, however, feared that the newcomers' Old World culture would provoke an anti-Semitic backlash. So they established charities, schools and social organizations to promote quick adaptation to the British way of life. They also encouraged new arrivals to whitewash their houses frequently and use disinfectants liberally.

By the time the Wolfsohns arrived in Manchester, more than half its Jews were cabinetmakers, water proofers, slipper makers, tailors, dressmakers and glaziers, trades many had learned at their fathers' knees. Samuel, now nearly 40 years old, was ready for change, he not only anglicized his surname to Woolfson, but together with his wife Jeanette, opened a fish and poultry stall.

Fish and poultry were traditionally marketed together. Many fishmongers also sold rabbits and game for that matter, but not Woolfson. He kept *kosher*. Still, despite his limited stock, his new calling held promise. Since consignments of fresh fish had begun arriving to landlocked Manchester by rail from the North Sea port of Grimsby in 1848, consumption had risen considerably. So had profits.

Although people frequented markets once or twice a week to stock up on perishables, few immigrants purchased the fancy 'Fried and Stewed Fish, Fine Smoked Salmon [or] Fine new Anchovies. …' regularly advertised in *The Jewish Chronicle*. Most opened their festive meals with traditional, economical *gefilte* fish.

After years of policing Sheffield, Woolfson could now finally enjoy *Shabbes* at home with Jeanette and their six children, three of whom, Annie, Henry, and Fanny, were born in Manchester.

Basch continued making cloth caps. He probably worked at home, utilizing the lower floor as his workshop, the attic as a storeroom where caps were aired, and the middle floor as living quarters. Although Manchester's cap market was much larger than that of Sheffield, here too he could barely earn a living. Finally, his poverty became too much too bear. In 1873, like millions of East Europeans before and after, he and his family sailed to the legendary gold-paved streets of New York. This time, however, the Woolfsons stayed behind.

After Samuel passed away in 1885, Jeanette continued running their fish and poultry business on her own. Yet the family could not make ends meet. By 1891, her daughters worked as domestics and one of her sons apprenticed to a cabinetmaker.

Another, Isaac, after labouring for a while as a 'mechanized tailor', became a water proofer at a rubber and leatherworks in Salford, a Manchester suburb. Through a process developed by Charles Mackintosh, he painted cloth with vulcanized Indian rubber, turning out waterproof outerwear, a popular commodity in that damp, rainy city.

Ever one to help a fellow Jew, Isaac found time to tutor English to new arrivals. According to family lore, he also once lent an acquaintance, Michael

Marks of Leeds, the tidy sum of five pounds. Presumably that helped this budding entrepreneur establish his famous penny bazaar, which eventually became Marks & Spencer.

Lewis, another Woolfson son, worked as a glazier, which required nothing more than a cutting diamond and a single pane of glass. He was blond and, apparently, given his English birth and his broad Yorkshire accent, often taken for a Gentile. Once while repairing a window for a Jewish woman, she cursed him out in Yiddish, certain that he had no idea what she was saying. When he had finished the job, he turned and, in Yiddish, wished her all the woes she'd wished on him.

After Jeanette's death in about 1903, her sons expanded the poultry business, which they continued until the 1950s.

Shimon Frais believes that his ancestor, Samuel Woolfson, had many merits. His descendants, who still live in Manchester and across the UK, range in observance from traditional to ultra-orthodox. No one has 'married out'. Yet none bear the name Wolfsohn or Woolfson.

With thanks to Shimon Frais, great-great-grandson of Samuel and Jeanette Woolfson.

Documents

Vital Records
Isaac Wolfsohn, Births registered in April-May-June 1862, 9c/324, *England and Wales Civil Registration Indexes*, GRO.
Itzig [Isaac] Basch, *Jewish Death and Household Registers, 1817-1845*, microfilm 1271465/203, LDS Library.
Jacob Basch-Emma Marsden, Marriages registered in January-February-March 1855, 9c/396, *England and Wales Civil Registration Indexes*, GRO.
Samuel Wolfsohn-Jeanette Basch , Marriages registered in July-Aug-Sept 1861, 9c/475, *England and Wales Civil Registration Indexes*, GRO.
Samuel Woolfson, death record, 140 [?] , 14 December 1885. GRO.

Census records
Jacob Basch household, RG9, 3482/ 29, TNA.
Samuel Wolfson [sic] household, RG9, 3482/34, TNA.
Samuel Wolfsohn household, RG11, 3991/94, TNA.

Correspondence
Email, 3 January 2003, Philip Lewin to Shimon Frais, referencing Itzig Basch.
Email, January 2003, Philip Lewin to Shimon Frais, referencing Wolf Samuel Wolfsohn.

Other

Basch, PRO HO3/51, *England, Alien Arrivals,* TNA.

Police Conduct and Commendation Books, 1831–1913, SY 295/3/1, Sheffield Archives and Local Studies, Sheffield, Yorkshire, UK.

S. Wolfson [sic], PRO HO3/88, *England, Alien Arrivals,* TNA.

Bibliography

Ballin, Neville David, *The Early Days of Sheffield Jewry 1760–1900,* Sheffield: publisher not noted, 1986.

Bermant, Chaim, *Troubled Eden*, New York: Basic Books, Inc., 1970.

Bowles M A, C. E. B., editor, Journal of the Derbyshire Archaeological and Natural History Society, Vol. 28-29, London & Derby: Bemrose & Sons, Ltd., 1906–07. http://archive.org/details/journalofderbysh28derb Retrieved 31 March 2012.

Elbogen, Ismar, *A Century of Jewish Life,* German, Moses Hadas, translator, Philadelphia: The Jewish Publication Society of America, 5707-1946.

Gartner, Lloyd P., *The Jewish Immigrant in England 1870-1914,* London & Portland, Oregon: Vallentine Mitchell, 2001.

'Great Britain; Riot in Sheffield – The Miners' Strike – Its Cause', *The New York Times,* 17 August 1869:1.

Harrison, Samuel, *A Complete History of the Great Flood at Sheffield on March 11 & 12, 1864,* Sheffield: S Harrison, 1864. http://books.google.com/ Retrieved 19 January 2011.

Heinz and Thea Ruth Skyte, 'Our Family: The History of the Jews of Neustadt near Pinne'. http://www.rijo.homepage.t-online.de/pdf/en_de_ju_sky50101.pdf Retrieved 19 January 2011.

Leader, R. E., *Reminiscences of Sheffield in the Eighteenth Century,* Sheffield: Sheffield Independent Press, 1901. http://archive.org/details/sheffieldineigh00leadgoog Retrieved 22 January 2011.

'Magisterial Proceedings, Sheffield, Monday, Systematic Robberies', *Sheffield and Rotherham Independent*, 26 November 1861: page unknown, Special Collections Department, University of Sheffield Western Bank Library.

'Notices', *The London Gazette*, 18 May 1869:2927.

Scola, Roger and Alan Armstrong, *Feeding the Victorian City: The Food Supply of Manchester, 1770–1870,* Manchester: Manchester University Press, 1992. http://books.google.com/ Retrieved 10 January 2011.

Slater, Isaac, compiler, printer, and publisher. *Slater's Directory of Manchester & Salford,* Manchester, 1886: 494. http://www.historicaldirectories.org Retrieved 1 April 2012.

'Synagogue Chambers, Figtree Lane, Sheffield 18th Dec., 1859-5620, To the Editor of The Jewish Chronicle', *The Jewish Chronicle,* 30 December 1859: 1.

'Trades' Unions and the Sheffield Murder', *The New York Times,* 8 July 1867: 1.

White, William, *General Directory of the Town, Borough and Parish of Sheffield.* Sheffield: Robert Leader, 1856: 61. http://www.historicaldirectories.org Retrieved 1 April 2012.

Williams, Bill, *The Making of Manchester Jewry,* Manchester: Manchester University Press, 1985.

Zangwill, Israel, *Children of the Ghetto,* Detroit, Michigan: Wayne State University Press, 1998. http://books.google.com/Retrieved 24 August 2011.

Chapter 5

Isidore S. Donn

Vilna, Russian Empire to London
1876

My heart is in the east, and I in the uttermost west –
How can I find savour in food? How shall it be sweet to me?
Yehuda HaLevi (c1085–-c1141).

Isidore Donn, in his short life, spanned the worlds of Victorian art, British society and Zionism. He was born in Vilna (today Vilnius, Lithuania), a city which, under the influence of Rabbi Eliyahu, the *'Gaon* of Vilna', was known for both rabbinical scholarship and its opposition to *Hasidus*. Also a centre of Jewish Enlightenment, printing and publishing, the city was one of the most influential Jewish cultural cities in Eastern Europe.

Although a selection of Vilna Governorate records have survived, no reference to Isidore's mother, Esther née Donn, have come to light. Moreover, since neither relevant marriage nor emigration records have been found, the original surname of his father Solomon Price remains unknown.

Although personal details of their youth remain elusive, Solomon and Esther lived through tumultuous times.

When both were about 20 years old, Tsar Alexander II, influenced by the abolitionist movement in the United States, freed more than twenty-three million serfs. Many Russians objected that their land grants were not only too small to sustain them, but were also heavily taxed, so tensions grew. Over a hundred demonstrations swept Vilna alone. To contain them, the Tsar instituted martial law.

Yet Vilna, well served by road and rail, was buzzing with commerce and industry. Jews supplied local markets with cattle, fowl, eggs, timber, leather, tobacco and pig bristles, which they purchased in surrounding villages. Merchants shipped locally-made products, including gloves and clothing, across the Russian Empire. Jews also laboured as goldsmiths, jewellers, hat makers, tailors, candlestick makers, shoemakers, cabinetmakers, watchmakers, tinsmiths and blacksmiths.

As more and more craftsmen streamed into town, however, competition increased, wages plummeted and poverty spread. Families were often forced to share single, dark, dank cellar rooms together.

Uprisings against the emancipation of the serfs, as well as conscription into the Imperial Russian army, swept the Empire in 1863. After crushing the rebellion, the Tsar imprisoned thousands of rebels and exiled or executed hundreds more. He then not only levied heavy taxes against the Jews, but also held them subject to secular, not rabbinical, law. Also, to promote Russification, he banned Polish and its Latin alphabet, proclaimed Russian the official language, and founded free Russian-language schools.

Several seasons of failed crops followed, which led to widespread famine. In 1868, when Isidore was 4, Sarah 3, Rachel 1, and Esther was expecting her fourth child, cholera swept the country, killing many and further weakening the economy. Many survivors, no longer able to earn a living, sought better lives elsewhere.

By the time the Prices left Vilna in 1876, they had five children under the age of twelve. Overland travel to North Sea ports, though it cut maritime time and costs considerably, required additional documentation to leave Russia legally. So they probably headed north by rail to the port cities Libau (today Liepja, Latvia) or Riga (also in Latvia), which lay within the Empire. Baltic boats and screw-steamers customarily docked along Britain's east coast, at Grimsby, Hull or London.

The family initially settled in Brick Lane at London's East End, an area known for its mean dwellings, gutters piled with refuse, squalling children, thievery and debauchery. Crowding was common, with multiple families often sharing single rooms.

Many young Jews, observed social investigator Richard Rowe, naturally sought diversion from everyday realities, flocking

> to the theatre, the singing-room, or the dancing-room, play cards, or dominoes, or bagatelle in low coffee-houses, or gamble by tossing on tables muffled to prevent the chink of the falling coin from being heard outside.

Gas-light illuminates the squalor and destitution of the streets,

> … gas-works' furnaces give out their infernal glow, kindling the air above and around into a core of lurid light, and painting bloody

gleams and weirdly fantastic shadows on the neighbouring buildings … dimly seen through the … gas-lit dust, and smoke, and mist hanging and dancing above like motes in the sunbeams, and the shrill or hoarse cries of the costermongers piercing the hum of many voices like sea-gulls screaming over murmuring waves …

Solomon Price may have laboured in a workshop or hawked produce from a market stall or barrow to support his growing family. When Helen, their sixth child, arrived in 1880, their home became even more crowded. The following year, the family left London for Leeds, a Yorkshire market town with over five hundred Jewish families.

Although they probably sought a house with more room, they settled at Vandyke Street, in Leylands, a square mile of dark courtyards and narrow, neglected cobble-stoned passageways edged by tiny back-to-back two-storied houses, noxious factories, leather works and a brewery.

From 1882 on, this area, notorious for its violence and immorality, swelled with refugees fleeing Polish and Russian persecution. Many of them, lured by the town's expanding clothing industry, became spinners, dyers, weavers, button-hole makers or pressers.

Solomon, by his own definition, was a designer and artist. His medium, however, possibly furniture, clothing, or jewellery, remains a mystery. Although one of his sons, Inman, was still in school, his teenage daughters, Sarah and Rachel, were already working as 'tailoresses'. When Daniel, his eighth child, arrived in 1882, overcrowding may not have posed a problem. Only seven children were living at home.

Isidore, an artist like his father, had remained behind in London's East End. The 17-year-old, possibly born Isaac or Israel, had both anglicized his name and adopted his mother's maiden name, Donn. Isidore Donn may have supported himself with a loan from the Jewish Board of Guardians or by peddling his sketches.

While Britain's working classes patronized popular music halls, public houses and sporting events, its upper and middle classes enjoyed attending concerts and visiting art galleries. Art, in Victorian England, was a highly respectable calling.

In addition to drawing, Isidore probably befriended his East End neighbours, many of whom, scarred in body and soul, had fled recent religious persecution.

Although Jews suffered anti-Semitism repeatedly over the ages, only in the nineteenth century did a movement to return to Zion, the Land of Israel, gain popularity. In July 1882, writes historian Ismar Elbogen, a band of enthusiastic, assimilated Russian university students banded together.

Recent

> tragic events had stirred them deeply and had aroused their Jewish consciousness; but they could see only one possible meaning in their being Jews, and that was to journey to the land of their fathers and there to work the soil with their hands. The idea took fire and the number of their adherents grew to 525; all wished to abandon their studies, emigrate to Palestine, and there establish model colonies on cooperative principles and so offer a solution not only for the Jewish problem but for the social problem generally as well.

A few months later, Leon Pinsker of Odessa published *Auto-Emancipation,* urging Jews to create a country for themselves. From then on, Jewish emigration to the Land of Israel began in earnest.

By 1885, while promoting the establishment of a Jewish homeland, and honing his artistic skills, Isidore apparently developed close connections with the staff of *The Jewish Chronicle.* From then on, this London-based newspaper, which was founded in 1841, featured many of his achievements.

In March, for example, it noted that Mr Isidore S. Donn,

> a young Jewish artist of great promise has just executed a life-like, faithful portrait in crayon of Mr Gladstone. The excellence of the portrait is proved for the fact that Mrs Gladstone has purchased it; and has written a letter to Mr Donn (who is Russian by birth) expressing her pleasure with it, and wishing him success.

Isidore's Mr Gladstone was none other than the prime minister of the United Kingdom. Reports of his portrait ran in the *Birmingham Daily Post, The Leeds Mercury* and the *North Wales Chronicle* as well.

Isidore evidently not only conceived and created this work, but also, on its completion, contacted the Prime Minister, then alerted the London press. Or did he?

Isidore had recently begun attending public classes at the National Art Training School in South Kensington, London (today Britain's Royal College of Art). There he apparently came under the wing of one of its instructors, sculptor Felix Martin Miller (1820–1908). Perhaps Miller, taking his protégé in hand, had orchestrated both the Gladstone sale and its subsequent publicity. Thereafter, Isidore often painted portraits of public figures.

Miller moved in royal social circles. One of his most famous works, for example, was a bust of Queen Victoria's daughter-in-law, Princess Alexandra. According to family lore, Isidore, possibly through Miller's good graces, became friendly with Princess Alexandra's son, Albert, Duke of Clarence.

The young man not only painted the Duke's portrait in oil, relates his family, but was also knighted by the Queen in gratitude.

By 1888, Isidore had joined *Kadima,* a Zionist organization that met at Tenter Building, Spitalfields, where Huguenot weavers had once stretched cloth on 'tenterhooks' to dry. Its members, in addition to organizing English lessons for 'greenies', also presented lectures like 'The Rising Hope of Israel', 'The Jewish Polish Golden Age' and 'Loyalty of Jews to Their Respective Countries'. Isidore lectured at least once, describing Jewish life from the death of the Roman emperor Hadrian to the death of Julian. He rose quickly in the organization's ranks. Following a successful concert to benefit the *Kadima* Library in August 1888, 'the chairman, Mr. I. S. Donn, reminded the audience of the great value which a library of Jewish history and literature had for foreign Jews.'

While his passion for Jewish nationalism was growing, Isidore supported himself by giving art lessons. In October and November 1888, he ran identical advertisements in *The Jewish Chronicle*.

ART.— LESSONS IN DRAWING by
an efficient master holding several
certificates from the [unintelligible] and Art Depart-
ments. Moderate terms. Good references.
Address Mr. I.S. Donn, National Art School
South Kensington, S.W.

The artist apparently received heartening responses. Within a year, he was able to leave Princes Street for better quarters at Brick Lane, Spitalfields.

In 1890, Isidore was elected to the provisional committee of the local 1,026-member *Chovevei Zion,* 'Lovers of Zion'. This international association, considered the forerunner of the Zionist movement, encouraged Jewish agricultural colonization of *Eretz-Yisroel*, the Land of Israel, through fund-raising and immigration. Its members, though promoting Hebrew as a living language and raising the moral and intellectual status of Israel, also pledged to obey the laws of the lands in which they lived.

Isidore had learned Biblical Hebrew in his early years in Vilna. Yet at Flowers of Zion, an East-End Zionist youth group, he probably taught Modern Hebrew, which had recently been revived by Eliezer Ben Yehuda. Classes were held three evenings a week in the Suwalk Synagogue, at Hanbury Street, Spitalfields.

In 1891, Isidore, along with a number of other Jewish artists, exhibited works at the 12th exhibition of the Institute of Painters in Oil Colours, Piccadilly. One of his oils, in which 'the flush of evening irradiates the sky, and shows up the line of distant hills, whilst a wooded slope makes up the

Better quarters, Brick Lane, Spitalfields. *Shimon Frais*

foreground', was entitled 'The Last Hill that Parleys With the Setting Sun'. This phrase may mean nothing to readers today. A hundred years ago, however, everyone would have recognized it as a quote from a popular poem by Wordsworth.

In 1892, Isidore was formally accepted to the National Art Training School, an institution that qualified art teachers and provided a focus for national art education. Its students studied geometry and perspective; architectural, freehand and mechanical drawing; painting in tempura, water colour and oil, as well as modelling, moulding and casting. Their drawing, painting and modelling classes explored both still-life and figural techniques.

When he applied for British naturalization a few months later, sculptor Felix Martin Miller, his artistic mentor, was one of his character references.

In 1893, Isidore's friends and patrons viewed 'a fine collection of portraits' of leading public figures at his new tenement studio at St John's Wood, a fashionable area popular with authors, artists and craftsmen. Nor did Isidore neglect his religious roots. He maintained ties with the Bryanston Road Synagogue, a branch of the Bevis Marks Spanish and Portuguese Synagogue, which was within walking distance.

In 1893, too, Isidore evidently joined the newly-formed Jewish Historical Society of England, which offered lectures on a wide range of topics relating to Anglo-Jewish history.

As Zionist groups sprang up around the world, proposals for representative flags arose as well. Many featured traditional Jewish symbols, like ramping Lions of Judah, blue Stars of David, gold stars forming Stars of David, or twelve stars representing the Twelve Tribes of Israel. All were set against white backgrounds.

Isidore, ardent artist and Zionist, also rose to the challenge. Journalist Jacob de Haas, an early leader of the British Zionist movement, reveals that

> The origin of the now-accepted Jewish flag – two bars of light blue with a white center filled with a Shield of David – is not clear. Isidor [sic] S. Donn, a Russian Jewish artist, who resided in London, made the first flag we ever saw. That was in 1893 in London. Donn claimed to have originated it and stated that the colors were based on Biblical authority and the stripes copied from the tallith (praying shawl).

In 1894, *The Jewish Chronicle* announced that though

> Mr Isidore S. Donn, whose name must now be added to the list of Jewish artists in England, has only been settled in his studio at St

for a Certificate of Naturalization (which Memorial is now produced and shown to us respectively and marked with the letter "A") and that according to the best of our knowledge, information and belief the statements made therein by the said *Isidore Sydney Donn* ——— true in substance and in fact. ——— are severally and respectively

8. And we the said *James Freeman, Abraham White, John Hall and Felix Martin Miller* ——— Spanders do further jointly and severally declare that we are not the Solicitors or Agents, nor is either of us the Solicitor or Agent of the said *Isidore Sydney Donn* ——— and we jointly and severally make this solemn declaration, conscientiously believing the same to be true and by virtue of the provisions of the Statutory Declaration Act, 1835.

Isidore Sydney Donn

John Hall *Abraham White*

James Freeman

Felix Martin Miller

Declared by the said Isidore Sydney Donn Abraham White and James Freeman at 3 Bishopsgate Street without in the City of London this 17th day of May 1892. Before me Wot. Whittington Commissioner for oaths

Declared by the said Felix Martin Miller at the National ... in the County of London this 18th day of May 1892. Before me Wot. Whittington Commissioner for oaths.

Declared by the said John Hall at 3 Bishopsgate Street without in the City of London this 20th day of May 1892 Before me Wot. Whittington Commissioner for oaths

Signatures, Isidore Sydney Donn Naturalization Application.

John's Wood during the last nine months; he is … represented by several portraits and two nude studies … including one of a little boy in a velvet tunic … whilst a small brownish red chalk head is instinct with life and feeling, and particularly pleasing.

That same year, he attended 'Constantinople', a show benefiting the Hammersmith and Kensington Synagogue Building Fund. Together with *Sephardi* patrons, he also contributed five pounds sterling to the building fund for a future Spanish and Portuguese Jews' congregation.

He also responded, in print, to an article published in *The Jewish Chronicle*, encouraging members of *Chovevei Zion* to fulfil the Biblical prophecy of returning to historic Palestine, the Land of Israel.

Aug 17, 1894

CHOVEVEI ZION
SIR—Every lover of Zion will re-echo the wish of Mr Wolf Miller in last Friday's Jewish Chronicle … Rishon Lezion, Zichron Yakab, and other colonies were established without any Firman [royal decree issued by a sovereign of the Ottoman Empire]. We must watch for the opportunity without looking for needless securities, but meanwhile collect funds without spending anything outside the scheme we contemplate – establishing an Anglo-Jewish Colony in Palestine.

He concludes with a Hebrew quote, 'Yet I will gather others to Him, besides those of Him that are gathered.' (Isaiah 56:8)

On the following *Simchas Torah*, the holiday that celebrates both the conclusion and beginning of the annual *Torah* reading cycle, Isidore received the honour of beginning Genesis at the Bryanston Road Synagogue.

Within weeks, he also opened an evening of songs and poetry organized by the *Bnei Zion* Association, an offshoot of *Kadima*. Members were trying a 'new method of propaganda', an artistic way of introducing Zionism to immigrant masses far more concerned with socialism, trade unionism and religious observance. Everything was well-received, especially the song describing 'the persecutions and sufferings of the Jews … The Hall was crowded to excess and the various items of the programme were greatly appreciated.'

By 1895, Isidore had become Commander of the Western *Bnei Zion* Association. That June, he presented a lecture entitled 'Israel – Retrospective and Perspective'. In it, he pointed out recent non-Jewish recognition of the value of Mosaic sanitary, dietary and legal codes.

'Constantinople' Benefit Performance, 1894. *The Jewish Chronicle*

Shortly afterwards, Isidore participated in the 13th Autumn Exhibition at the Manchester Art Gallery. He exhibited 'The Last Hill that Parleys with the Setting Sun,' offering it for a goodly sum, 19 pounds and 19 shillings (19 guineas). By this time, indicative of his artistic success, he had settled in stylish 16 North Audley Street, Grosvenor Square, London.

That November, Theodor Herzl arrived in London. The previous year, the charismatic, Paris-based journalist had witnessed the conviction of Jewish officer Alfred Dreyfus for treason, followed by mass anti-Semitic demonstrations. As cries of 'Death to the Jews!' rang through the streets, this emancipated Jew realized that his people's attempts to assimilate into European society would never overcome innate anti-Semitism. The only solution, he came to believe, was the creation of an independent Jewish State.

In 1896, Herzl's article, 'A "Solution of the Jewish Question"', appeared in *The Jewish Chronicle*.

The Jewish question still exists. It would be useless to deny it. It exists wherever Jews live in perceptible numbers. Where it does not exist, it is carried by Jews in the course of their migrations. We naturally move to those places where we are not persecuted, and there our presence produces persecution. … In countries where we have lived for centuries we are still cried down as strangers … . This is my message fellow Jews! Neither fable nor fraud! Every man may test its truth for himself, for every man will carry within him a portion of the Promised Land –one in his head, another in his arms, another in his acquired possessions. We shall live at last, as free men, on our own soil, and die peacefully in our own home.

Yet when Herzl presented these ideas to the Maccabeans, a British association of Anglo-Jewish artists, writers and professionals, he was received unfavourably. Many in the audience feared that Herzl's impassioned ideas would lead to increased anti-Semitism. The poor Jews of Whitechapel, East End, however, greeted him with enthusiasm. They

were of many birthplaces – Austria, Holland, Poland, Russia, Germany, Italy, Spain – yet felt themselves of no country and of one. Encircled by the splendors of modern Babylon, their hearts turned to the East, like passion-flowers seeking the sun. Palestine, Jerusalem … the Holy Land were magic syllables to them, the sight of a coin struck in one of Baron Edmund's colonies filled their eyes with tears … .

All the while, Isidore continued to ply his art. In July 1896, he exhibited 'an admirable likeness, in oils, [of] Dr. Strauss in his rabbinical robes', in the Free Library in Bradford, West Yorkshire. Since Bradford lies but a few miles from Leeds, perhaps family members attended.

Two months later, Isidore attended a ceremony at the Literary Society of the New Briggate Synagogue in Leeds to honour a visiting dignitary. He did not arrive alone, reported *The Jewish Chronicle,* 'Above the seat occupied by the distinguished guest,' '… the Russian Eagle, and the Jewish National Flags presented by … Mrs Isidore Donn, fluttered from the walls.'

Isidore had married.

The Zionist movement continued to gain momentum. In 1897, the Maccabeans toured Palestine and Herzl convened the first Zionist Congress in Basel, Switzerland. It was a productive time for Isidore too. After studying art in Paris, he and his wife toured Rome and Florence.

Somewhere along the way, Isidore contracted a fatally high fever. In January 1898, at Villefranche-sur-Mer, France, the 33-year-old, with his wife Florence (S)Hort at his side, breathed his last. He was laid to rest in the Jewish cemetery of Nice, overlooking the Mediterranean.

Two days later, *The Jewish Chronicle* published a brief obituary. It notes his artistic achievements, then concludes, 'He took a great personal interest in the Zionist Movement.' *The Jewish World* adds

> By his death we have lost one of the first active Zionists in England – the founders of the National Society 'Kadima' later called 'Bnei Zion'. … To record all that he has done for the movement is impossible. His ideas and speeches were most logical. In one, in which I can remember from one of his debates with a non-believer was 'Has it ever been heard that one who is dangerously ill should wish to be poisoned as to relieve him of his [suffering], no one wishes to die, no matter how ill one might be he still has hope that he will recover from his illness gladly takes the medicine to be cured.'

Death certificate, Donn, Isidore Sidney.

Isidore's namesake. *Census Returns of England and Wales, 1901.*

[Mr Donn's thoughts] can be applied to the Jewish People. The Jews are spiritually weak but should not and dare not give up hope, but they must renew their courage and strive to be a United Nation in their own land 'Palestine'.

Perhaps Isidore and Florence did reach Palestine as well. Perhaps they 'took the crazy little train that pants over the single line to the Holy City', [winding] in and out among the mountains of Judea; ever rising steadily …' to Jerusalem. Perhaps he contracted malaria in that swampy Ottoman backwater.

Perhaps the couple then hastened to Villefranche, which, as a favoured winter residence of British royalty and the wealthy, promised quality medical care. Or, if his death certificate is correct, they had made sunny Nice, a painter's paradise, their temporary home.

The following year, Isidore's uncle Barnet, following Jewish tradition, named his newborn son Isidore. Over the years, several other relatives did the same.

75

More than a century has passed since Isidore's death. None of his paintings, as far as is known, have survived. Yet his blue and white flag flutters over the Land of Israel.

With thanks to Shimon Frais, Isidore S. Donn's great-nephew, who immigrated to Israel in 1987.

Documents

Vital Records

Donn, Isidore Sidney, death certificate, 27 January 1898, Office of the Mayor of Villefranche, District of Nancy, France, Departmental Archives of Alpes Maritime.

Price-Donn, Esther, Deaths registered in April-May-June 1901, 9b/286, *England and Wales Civil Registration Indexes,* GRO.

Census Records

Solomon Price household, RG11, 4517/85, TNA

Ester P. Donn household, RG13, 4221/22, TNA.

Barnet Dawn household, RG12, 3689/7, TNA.

Barnard Donn household, RG13, 4221/22, TNA.

Eli Fraize household, RG14, 26951, TNA.

Esther Price household, RG12, 3689/53, TNA.

Other

Isidore Sydney Donn, Naturalization Application, 20 May 1892, HO144/339/B12503, TNA.

'Thirteenth Autumn Exhibition 1895', Corporation of Manchester Art Gallery, photocopied pamphlet in possession of Steven Frais, Beit Shemesh, Israel.

Bibliography

'A"Solution of the Jewish Question"', *The Jewish Chronicle,* 17 January 1896: 13.

'ART-LESSONS in DRAWING', *The Jewish Chronicle*, 12 October 1888:3.

'ART-LESSONS in DRAWING', *The Jewish Chronicle*, 16 November 1888: 2.

'B'nei Zion Association', *The Jewish Chronicle,* 26 October 1894:14.

'Bradford', *The Jewish Chronicle*, 31 July 1896:17.

'Chovevi [sic] Zion', *The Jewish Chronicle,* 17 August 1894:5.

De Haas, Jacob. *Theodor Herzl: a Biographical Study,* Chicago and New York: Leonard, 1927. http://books.google.com Retrieved 15 August 2011.

'Dr Dembo's Visit to Leeds', *The Jewish Chronicle,* 11 September 1896: 17.

Elbogen, Ismar, *A Century of Jewish Life*, German, Moses Hadas, translator, Philadelphia: The Jewish Publication Society of America, 5707-1946.

'Flowers of Zion Society', *The Jewish Chronicle*, 21 November 1890:16.

'Gleanings', *Birmingham Daily Post,* 25 March 1885: 7.

'Great Benefit Performances', *The Jewish Chronicle*, 13 April 1894:10.

Greenbaum, Marsha, *The Jews of Lithuania: A History of a Remarkable Community 1316–1945*, Jerusalem, New York: Gefen, 1995.

'Institute of Painters in Oil Colours', *The Jewish World*, 2 November 1891: page unknown.

'Isidore S. Donn', *The Jewish Chronicle*, 11 February 1898:28.

'Kadima Association', *The Jewish Chronicle*, 27 January 1888:14.

'Kadima Association', *The Jewish Chronicle*, 10 August 1888:12.

Krausz, Ernest, *Leeds Jewry: Its History and Social Structure*, Cambridge: The Jewish Historical Society of England, 1964.

Levin, Dov, *The Litvaks: A Short History of the Jews of Lithuania*, Jerusalem: Yad VaShem, 2000.

'Mr Isidore S. Donn', *The Jewish Chronicle*, 11 February 1898: 28.

'Obituary', Isidore S. Donn, *The Jewish World*, ?? 1898, p. unknown.

'On Sunday Last', *The Jewish Chronicle*, 8 December 1893:6.

'On Tour in Palestine – Notes By the Way', *The Jewish Chronicle*, 30 April 1897:18-19.

'Portrait of Mr Gladstone', *North Wales Chronicle*, 4 April 1885:7.

Post Office London Directory, 1895, *Part 4: Trades & Professional Directory*. London: Kelly & Co Limited: 1599. http://www.historicaldirectories.org Retrieved 23 August 2011.

'Rejoicing of the Law', *The Jewish Chronicle*, 19 October 1894:20.

Rowe, Richard, 'Saturday Night at the East End, *1881',*

The Victorian Dictionary, Lee Jackson, compiler. http://www.victorianlondon.org/ Retrieved 7 July 2011.

'Round The Studios', *The Jewish Chronicle*, 6 April 1894:19.

'Spanish and Portuguese Jews' Congregation', *The Jewish Chronicle*, 8 June 1894:3.

'Portrait of Mr. Gladstone', *The Leeds Mercury*, 28 March, 1885:10.

'The Colonisation of Palestine', *The Jewish Chronicle*, 7 March 1890: 9.

The Saperia Family Website: Our History http://www.saperia.com/ Retrieved 11 July 2011.

'Western B'nei Zion', *The Jewish Chronicle*, 25 January 1895:11.

'Western B'nei Zion', *The Jewish Chronicle*, 7 June 1895:15.

Zangwill, Israel, *Children of the Ghetto*, Detroit, Michigan: Wayne State University Press, 1998. http://books.google.com/Retrieved 24 August 2011.

Chapter 6

Yekusiel 'Ksiel' Pelikan

Krakow, Austro-Hungarian Empire to London, c1877

Thou shalt not wear a mingled stuff, wool and linen together
Deuteronomy 22:11.

Ksiel Pelikan was born in Tarnow, a town in Galicia, a crescent-shaped area that today spans the Polish and Ukrainian borders. Initially, Galicianer Jews flourished culturally and prospered. In time, however, to stem economic competition with their non-Jewish neighbours, they were restricted to occupations that either served their communities, like butchers and tailors, or were marginal, like tavern keepers, distillers and peddlers. Because Jews were educated, they were also appointed stewards and tax collectors for vast Polish feudal estates, thus earning the resentment of their neighbours.

Jews first reached Tarnow in the mid-1400s. Initially, they dwelt along 'Jew Street', outside the city walls, trading in grain or wines from Hungary and Russia. By the late 1500s, they also distilled and sold lucrative spirits. Tarnow's ruling nobility, in addition to allowing them to earn a living, also protected their synagogue and cemetery from desecration.

By the eighteenth century, a handful of Jewish lawyers, physicians, musicians, industrialists and teachers were allowed to settle within Tarnow itself. Their small community supported a synagogue, some prayer houses, schools, cultural societies and a Jewish press

Austria annexed Galicia in 1772, in the First Partition of Poland. When Jozef II assumed power, in the spirit of tolerance, he granted Jews freedom of travel and a wider choice of occupations. To advance assimilation, however, he forbade use of Hebrew or Yiddish except in prayer, required Jewish children to attend secular schools, abolished communal autonomy, and banned traditional Jewish dress. In 1788, to promote national

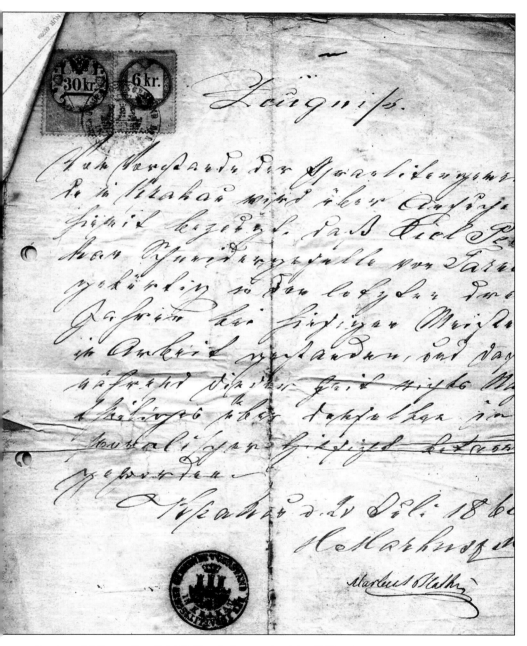

Testimonial Regarding Ksiel Pelikan's Apprenticeship, 1860. *Alex Pelican*

conscription and taxation, he required each Jewish family member 'without exception' to adopt a German surname for use on all legal documents.

During this era, hundreds of *Hasidic* rabbinic dynasties, attracting over 100,000 followers, arose in small, predominantly Jewish towns across Galicia, called *shtetls*. *Shtetl* life revolved around the home, the synagogue and the marketplace.

Most Jews struggled to earn enough money during the week to buy chickens or fish for *Shabbes*. They augmented their meagre incomes by peddling homemade cheese or eggs, or renting out their horses and wagons on market day. Others split and sold firewood, cobbled shoes, or combed the neighbouring villages for bargains like windfalls of ripe plums or cheap sheepskins.

Joseph Margoshes, who was born in Tarnow, recalls that the town

> had a reputation across all of Galicia and the voice of the Torah was heard there twenty-four hours a day … . Virtually all the frum Jews of Tarnow were adherents of the Sanzer [Halberstam] Rebbe … . [Yet] There were [also] large numbers of misnagdim and ordinary frum Jews. There were also a lot of educated people who did not think much of rebbes. Or the excesses of their followers – drinking, blind faith in their leaders, and their belief in miracles.

Many educated Tarnower Jews, embraced rational *Haskalah,* Jewish Enlightenment. This movement, which originated in eighteenth century Germany, furthered Jewish assimilation by promoting Hebrew over Yiddish, and modern secular studies and philosophy in place of religion.

By the 1830s, when Ksiel was born, Tarnow's Jews had settled around its market square, where many hawked their goods. Visiting Scottish missionaries remarked on

> their high fur-caps … the rich head-dress of the women, and the small round velvet caps of the boys …. In the bazaar, Jews were selling skins, making shoes, and offering earthenware for sale; and the sign-boards of plumbers, masons, painters, and butchers, all bore Jewish names.

Jews also contributed to Tarnow's thriving clothing, metal, ceramic, wood, hat-making and fur industries.

Just the same, they lived an uneasy truce with the local peasantry, broken by occasional beatings, robberies and accusations of blood libel.

When Ksiel was 11 years old, reveals *The Voice of Jacob*, a lad nearly his age, weary of the short allowances and ill treatment to which he was subjugated by his master, absconded eight days before Passover. Either malice against the Jews, or the superstition inherited from the middle ages, or (a more probable motive,) his being deeply indebted to the Jewish merchants here, induced … the authorities … [to] make a diligent search in all Jewish homes, since, 'according to well known facts' he had not the lightest doubt that the boy had been decoyed away by the Jews, secreted in some obscure place, and reserved for a Pascal offering. Imagine to yourself now the vaunted spirit of the nineteenth century, prevailing in Gallicia! … the succeeding night, all the avenues leading to the Jewish quarter were closed, and surrounded by a powerful military guard. … Several magistrates, accompanied by a body of police … forced their entrance into every house inhabited by Jews. Everything was overturned; cellars, garrets, even boxes and cupboards; nothing was spared. But all was vain; nowhere was a trace of Christian blood discovered. Meanwhile, the affair made a greater sensation everyday; and nothing was talked of but revenge against the 'Jewish vampires' ….

Ultimately, the boy, found in good health, was delivered to the proper authorities.

At the time, a number of Tarnowers supported an underground movement that furthered the struggle for Polish independence. In 1846, the year Ksiel celebrated his *Bar Mitzva,* local peasants, in support of the ruling Austrian government, destroyed manorial estates and slaughtered more than a thousand local, rebellious noblemen leaders and their families. Then, in a grand gesture, they presented the corpses to the Tarnow Town Council.

Tarnow's economy accelerated with the arrival of the railway. Yet between 1853 and 1855, wider Galicia suffered a major famine, the result of nearly a decade of poor crops. Ensuing malnutrition and poor sanitation led to 'The Great Cholera Epidemic', one of many outbreaks that periodically afflicted the area. Several hundred thousand people perished.

When he reached his twenties, Ksiel apprenticed to a local tailor. Since tailoring, which required only a needle and a bit of cloth, could be plied anywhere and provided a necessary commodity, it attracted many impoverished craftsmen.

In 1860 a committee of five master tailors attested, in florid German script, that

Ksiel Pelikan, a journeyman tailor born in Tarnow, during the period from the 2nd of Marsh [May] 1854 until April 30, 1857, did work with

81

the local master tailor, Schije Schmid, and, during this complete period, his behaviour was loyal, good and of morally good conduct, and we recommend him by all means. We … admit him to the list of journeymen.

Just days after receiving this testimonial, Ksiel and his wife, Rachel Blodek, daughter of peddler-merchant Herschel Blodek and Malka Gittel Etman, left Tarnow for Krakow, her home town.

Rev Robert Murray McCheyne, who made the same trip, recalls boarding

a Jewish carriage, driven by a Jew with a long beard … We accomplished this journey in perfect safety – being protected and carried forward by a divine hand. We slept every night for a few hours, and always in a Jewish khan, so that we were saved from many of those unpleasant adventures which sometimes take place in Polish inns.

Krakow, one of the oldest cities in historic Poland, was noted for its art, culture and architectural wonders. If the Pelikans glimpsed its ancient castle, cathedral, or famed university, however, it was probably from afar. Jews were confined to Krakow's Jewish Quarter, Kazimierz, their centre of religious and social life.

Visiting Scottish missionaries observed that

They follow all trades, and yet have no bread to eat. They are so poor that, out of all the Jews in the republic, there are not 10,000 who could afford to pay one shilling for a Hebrew Bible. Twelve families are often lodged in one room in winter, the floor being chalked out into so many portions, and a whole family huddled together in each, the children generally remaining in bed to keep themselves warm, as they have no clothes to defend them from the cold …

Within a week of his arrival in Krakow, journeyman-tailor Ksiel secured a second testimonial, in German script, signed by the President of the Jewish Community. This document, an identity card, summary of work experience and character reference all-in-one, probably eased his acceptance locally both personally and professionally.

Ksiel was naturally concerned about supporting his family. His dark-blond, brown-eyed wife was expecting their first child, Taube. Over the next two years, the couple welcomed two more daughters, Faigl Roze and Surel.

Although Ksiel was employed and his family thriving, times were troubled. In December 1862, reports *The Jewish Chronicle,*

Two [Kazimierz] Jews had a fight with two soldiers, and these getting the worst of it, called about fifty other soldiers to their assistance, who indiscriminately attacked all Jews they met, smashing windows, demolishing houses, and freely using their bayonets. The assailed bravely defended themselves with sticks and bludgeons. ... The riot continued for three hours, before three companies of soldiers ... succeeded in quelling the disturbance.

Malke, the Pelikans' fourth daughter, arrived in 1866, the year Austria, after losing the Austro-Prussian War, granted Galician Jews equal status. Thereafter, the community fared better, except for occasional robberies and beatings by the local peasantry. Yet their economic condition did not improve.

The following year, the Municipal Authority of Krakow granted Ksiel a license allowing him to work as a self-employed tailor in Kazimierz. Previously, he had probably worked in another's employ.

When Kazimierz and Krakow merged in 1868, its Jews were granted additional trade rights, along with freedom of movement. A few wealthier ones moved into Krakow proper, where they dealt in wine, textiles, feathers, timber and eggs. Most, however, remained in Kazimierz, within walking distance of their schools and synagogues. Many worked as grocers or haberdashers, dealing in leather, textiles, or clothing, or as carpenters, or like Ksiel, tailors. Others dealt in pig bristles and horsehair, which they purchased in neighbouring villages.

The Pelikans' fifth daughter, Leie, born that same year, succumbed to meningitis four years later. A son, Herschel, arrived soon after. Their next child, Chaja, appears twice in the 1873 Krakow Birth Index, under both Blodek and Pelikan.

This was not unusual. Many Eastern European couples married solely in Jewish tradition, 'under the *chuppa*'. Since they did not register their unions with civil authorities, their children legally retained their mothers' maiden names.

Some time after Chaja's birth, relates family chronicler Madeline (Rosenlicht) Wekselblatt in her diary, tragedy struck. The baby's mother, Rachel, 'died of cholera in an epidemic ... leaving six children motherless ... the eldest twelve years old, and a new born infant ... given to a Polish woman to nurse ...'

Although Wekselblatt's source was probably her own mother, Rachel's sister, she was known to embellish memories to avoid any whiff of scandal. Besides, adds Paul Auerbach, a Pelikan descendant, 'while we don't know exactly when Madeline Wekselblatt wrote her diary, it's safe to say that it was about 100 years after Rachel's death. Any way you slice it, that's a lot of time, and memories can fade.'

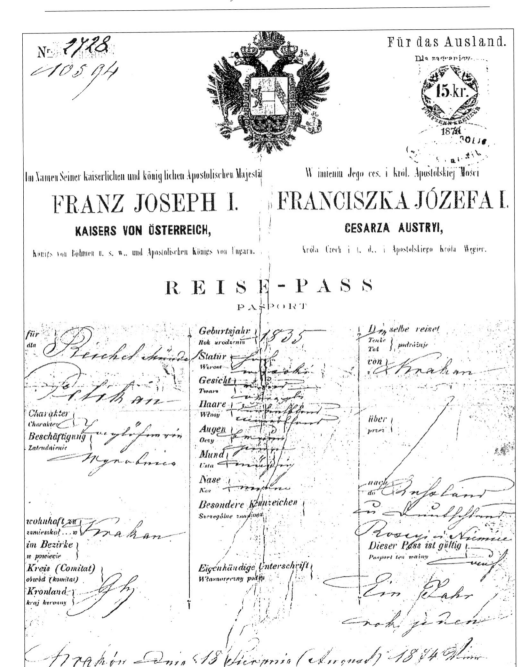

Reise-Passe, Reichel Mundel Pelikan, 1874. *Alex Pelican*

Still, the death of one's mother does not lend itself to fabrication. Moreover, 'Little Cholera' did indeed strike Galicia between 1873 and 1874.

In addition to Wekselblatt's handwritten notes, the family also owns two original *Reise-Passes*, florid internal identification cards granted 'In the Name of His Imperial and Royal Apostolic Majesty, Franz Joseph I, Emperor of Austria, King of Bohemia etc., and Apostolic King of Hungary'. These documents allowed traders, tourists and emigrants to travel from Krakow through Russia and Germany once within a year of their issue.

The time between applying for a *Reise-Passe* and actually receiving it is unknown. So when Rachel's *passe* arrived, in 1874, she may have already died.

Even if she had, Ksiel was apparently determined to emigrate as planned.

A week after receiving her *passe*, he, true to character, arranged a letter of recommendation from the Krakow Rabbinical Court.

Blessed be G-D. Let our words be liked by our brethren the children of Israel, them and their ancestors of compassionate hearts, on behalf of the bearer of this letter, the dear and virtuous Mr Yekusiel Pelikan … this man earned his own bread all his days as he is an artisan, always was honest and decent, eager to observe the word of G-D and willing to keep His commandments, and this last year his business has gone down and he is unable to support his children as there are many of them, and he has a baby daughter who needs a wet nurse which he can't afford. Therefore, he made up his mind to travel far away, perhaps he can find a place where he can make a living through his skills, and we here recommend that wherever he comes he should be welcome until he arrives at his destination, and every person should contribute a donation to him according to the financial ability bestowed upon him by G-D. As a result of this, G-D will bless you and bestow richness and prosperity upon your homes, and your righteousness will stand forever.

Although this document does not refer to his widowhood, mention of a daughter needing a wet nurse supports the theory that Rachel had already died.

Ksiel received his own *Reise-Passe* two years later, in October 1876. Just before it expired, he and his son Herschel left Krakow for good.

Emigrant Jews, travelling by foot, cart or rail toward Baltic ports like Bremen, Hamburg or Gdansk, naturally gravitated toward Jewish communities along the way. In Jewish tradition, those who respond to

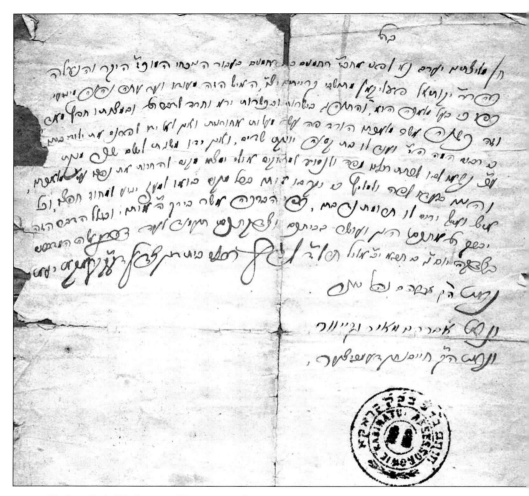

Krakau *Beth Din* Letter of Recommendation, 1874. *Alex Pelican*

rabbis' requests for aid to the needy earn merit in Heaven. So the Pelikans, along with *kosher* food, the opportunity for communal prayer, and provision for Sabbaths and holidays, surely received warm welcomes.

Although details of their departure and entry into the UK remain unknown, Wekselblatt records that on arrival, Ksiel married a 'beautiful English woman named Fannie Klein'. Her words, which were penned decades after the fact and a continent away, have never been verified.

Records do show, however, that, by 1881, Ksiel, now known as Alexander Pelikan, had married someone named Minnie. Family members, citing the similarity between the names 'Minnie' and 'Reichal Mündel', as Rachel appears on her *Reise-Passe,* wonder if these two women were actually one and the same.

Since both were born in Krakow in the mid-1830s, perhaps Rachel actually survived the epidemic, then emigrated to England ahead of her family. Perhaps her departure – rather than her death – created the need for a wet nurse. Perhaps Rachel's daughter Taube, unable to confront the pain of temporary maternal abandonment, fabricated death by cholera, later sharing this scenario with her daughter, Madeline.

To add to the mystery, documentation of Minnie and Alexander's marriage, religious or civil, has never been found. Nor is Minnie's maiden name known. Moreover, Pelikan's son Herschel, at her death years hence, claimed Minnie as his mother.

While Alexander had been tailoring by hand in Krakow, the Singer sewing machine, invented in 1851, and related innovations were mechanizing the trade in Britain. There, fashioning a waistcoat, lady's jacket or mantle, at least among Jewish tailors, was no longer a one-man enterprise from start to finish. It had become a highly efficient division of labour, determined by the size of the workshop.

Even 'greeners' with little needle experience could, within a short time, pick up the basic skills needed to operate sewing, cutting and braiding machines. If not, they could always work as basters, pressers, under pressers, fellers, buttoners or finishers.

Alexander, considering his experience, may have become a fixer, a tailor who, overseeing the work of others, earned the most money in the least hours. Yet tailoring, even for fixers, was precarious. Workshops constantly opened and closed. Hours were long, business was seasonal, and from 1881 onward, the steady arrival of Russian and Polish Jewish 'greeners', willing to work at all cost, kept wages low.

In 1881, Alexander 'Palakan' and Minnie, dubbed 'Millie' by their careless census enumerator, were living on Philip Street, in London's crowded St George-in-the-East. The Reverend Harry Jones, a resident himself, reveals that

> No one dreams of a carriage airing in this part of the East. Here I have never seen a coachman in a wig, or a footman in powder. I have never met a lady on horseback, or a 'Victoria' [a light four-wheeled horse-drawn carriage with a collapsible hood] and, though we go much about on foot, such a luxury as a crossing-sweeper is unknown. ... here the strain of work and sentiment of toil is continuous. ... We live much from hand to mouth. Every farthing has to be earned, and a sixpence is severely perceived to be worth six pennies.

Within four years of arrival, Alexander sent for Taube, Faigl, Surel and Malke, the children he had left behind, one by one. To wrest the baby Chaja from the arms of her Polish wet nurse, however, he had to take court action. Minnie, though snobbish about her Jewishness, frowned on newcomers who spoke Yiddish, wrestled with English or exhibited other 'typical' Jewish traits. So the children were soon known as Debora, Fanny, Sarah, Millie, Annie and Harry. Except for Annie and Harry who were still in school, the entire family laboured as tailors, seamstresses or furriers. With this combined effort, they evidently did well.

In 1882, when Debora, their daughter, married Albert Rosenlicht in New York City, Alexander and the entire family arrived briefly to celebrate the occasion.

He and Minnie returned to New York the following year to greet their first grandchild. This time, entertaining the possibility of staying, Alexander secured a well-paying tailoring job in Manhattan. In time, however, the couple decided that they preferred the English way of life, and left once more. The Wekselblatts never saw them again.

By 1888, Alexander owned a tailor shop at 31 Berners (today Henriques) Street, in St George-in-the-East. That year, an unknown assailant, later dubbed 'Jack the Ripper,' attacked a woman, his third victim, in a narrow yard between number 40, the noisy International Working Men's Educational Club, and 42 Berners Street. Between then and 1891, ten additional gruesome murders, all of young women and all perpetrated nearby, followed. The Pelikans must have feared not only the grip of the Ripper, but also the waves of anti-Semitism that spread in his wake.

By now, though most Berners Street tailor shops were small and turned out 'very common work', Alexander, by sub-contracting a handful of 'sweated' labourers, may have become his own master.

Indeed, wrote social reformer Beatrice Potter,

The ease with which a man may become a master is proverbial at the East End. His living-room becomes his workshop, his landlord or his butcher his security; round the corner he finds a brother Israelite whose trade is to supply pattern garments to take as samples of work to the wholesale house; with a small deposit he secures on the hire system both sewing machines and presser's table. Altogether it is estimated that with £1 in his pocket any man may rise to the dignity of a sweater. At first the new master will live on 'green' labour, will, with the help of his wife or some other relative, do all the skilled work that is needed. Presently, if the quantity of his work increases, or if the quality improves, he will engage a machinist, then a presser. His earnings are scanty, probably less than those of either of the skilled hands to whom he pays wages, and he works all hours of the day and night. But the chances of the trade are open to him; with indefatigable energy and with a certain measure of organizing power he may press forward into the ranks of the large employers ...

George R. Sims, social reformer and satirist, offers a tour of a 'sweated' tailor shop.

Let us enter a 'dwelling' workshop. It is a room nine feet square. In it fourteen people are at work. There is a coke fire, and seven or eight gas jets are burning. Ventilation there is none. The sweater is at work himself. Hollow-eyed, gaunt-visaged men and women are toiling in various ways. Some have a sewing machine, others are doing handwork. It is evening when we enter. The poor wretches have been at work since six o'clock in the morning. They will go on probably till midnight, for it is the season, and the sweater has his hands full. The wages these poor foreigners can earn by their ceaseless toil will perhaps be eight shillings at the week's end. For that they will work on Sunday also. All the gold of the Rothschilds could not tempt us to stay an hour in this place ... Let us hurry out into the air.

Decades earlier, many Jewish 'sweaters', those who had embraced socialist ideals in Tsarist Russia, strove to improve their working conditions by establishing trade unions. Due to members' differing customs, work methods and personal aims, however, most of their groups eventually splintered, split, then dissolved. By 1889, however, the Amalgamated Society of Tailors wielded great strength. When, on the heels of the Match Girls' Strike and the Great Dock Strike, it called a general strike, ten thousand Jewish needle workers responded.

The Jewish Chronicle supported their grievances.

they are compelled to work 15 to 16 hours consecutively, for a day's wage. For the first three days of the week they are mostly idle. It is generally on Thursday mornings that the men are taken on to work. They are then compelled to labour 'nearly every hour that the Almighty gives them' during Thursday and Friday, and are paid two days' wages. Having nothing whatsoever to do on the early days of the week, it can easily be understood that their lives become demoralised. Satan can always find plenty of work for idle hands to do. The homes of Jewish tailors – generally consisting of one or perhaps two dirty and ill-ventilated rooms, with the usual large number of small children … offer no attraction to them, and the workers loaf about the street-corners. In course of time they … are seduced into the more congenial premises of the Berners Street [Workingmen's Educational] Club. It is here they hear repeatedly dinned into their ears the hardships which they have to undergo, and are assured that the only panacea for the ills from which they suffer is Socialism. Is it any wonder that they are an easy prey for the Socialist agitator?

Indeed, tailors' trade meetings, which were usually conducted in Yiddish, often spiralled into ideological arguments among socialists, anarchists, and pro- and anti-Zionists. Yet their efforts eventually inspired needleworkers in Leeds, Manchester and other Jewish centres to strike as well.

Alexander remained observant all his life. In 1892, his name, spelled 'Palacan', appeared on a marble plaque marking the consecration of the New Road Synagogue, Whitechapel.

On *Simchas Torah*, he received the honour of *Chatan Torah*, reciting the concluding portion of Deuteronomy.

Minnie Pelikan, 59, succumbed to cancer in July 1897. Two and a half months later, Alexander, then over 60 years old, wed Jane Hyamson, the former Jane Lazarus, in a civil ceremony. She was a 44-year-old divorcee.

Their circumstances of their marriage – their age difference, their quick courtship, and Jane's marital status – were probably not as scandalous as they appear today. At the time, a divorcee in her mid-forties, with scant prospect of finding another husband, and an elderly widower, in need of a caretaker, were a likely pair.

When the 1901 census was taken, Alexander was sharing a spacious four-room home with three of his daughters on Union Street, Shoreditch. His recent bride, left unmentioned, was apparently out for the evening.

A decade later, when the next census

Alexander Pelikan. *Alex Pelican*

was taken, she was absent as well. What's more, genealogical searches for her whereabouts over these years have yielded no results. Alexander's summer-winter marriage, like the nagging Rachel-Minnie mystery, has long puzzled Pelikan descendants.

Then just as these words were about to go to press, Paul Auerbach, while sifting through one of the resources that continually become available online, made a startling discovery. An article in *Lloyd's Weekly Newspaper* reveals that in 1898,

> Alexander Pelican … was summoned … to police-court … for deserting his wife, who claimed maintenance in consequence; [Pelican] was nearly 63 years old, but the wife several years younger. They had, however, been married scarcely 12 months. There had been several quarrels … until during the absence of the wife one day the husband left, removing the household goods except … a bed, which was her property before the marriage … the husband refused to live again with the woman and offered five [pounds] a week [for her maintenance]. The wife said it was not enough, and alleged that her husband had allowed her 25 [pounds] a week for housekeeping money; had also paid the rent, and brought in every Saturday night three pints of whisky and some soda water for the weekly allowance. His income, therefore, was over 40 [pounds] a week …

Under oath, Pelikan swore that he only earned twelve pounds a week working part time for his son, to which his daughters added a small weekly sum. Harry, noting that his father was in feeble health, verified this. When the judge enquired if his father had revealed his income prior to his marriage to Jane,

> The son said he did not know, but that his father's last wife did not have as much money … His last wife? How many wives has he had? – the son said the present was the third wife … She knew his illness when she married him, but he wanted someone to look after him, and so he married a third time. But the third time is not always lucky …

Since Alexander married thrice, Rachel and Minnie could not have been one and the same. The mysteries of both Rachel-Minnie and his summer-winter marriage were solved.

Still, Auerbach admits to mixed feelings.

God's Noblest Work An Honest Man. *Raymond Montanjees*

While I have been doggedly searching for the truth, it's difficult to discover the painful direction that Alexander's life took after Minnie's death. This article ... poked fun at his having been married three times, but as we know, his first two wives died of terrible illnesses, cholera and cancer. The publication of that article, which reached a huge number of readers, must have been an enormous embarrassment to a religious man like Alexander. It's no wonder that Madeline [Wekselblatt] ... kept this story deeply buried (if she ever knew it at all).

Its positive aspect, if there is one, is the noble way in which Harry Pelican employed his enfeebled father and his daughters cared for him through the last fifteen years of his life.

Alexander died in August 1911. Lying beside Minnie in London's East End Plashet Cemetery, he remains

Deeply Mourned by His Sorrowing Children, Grandchildren & Relatives God's Noblest Work An Honest Man

With thanks to Alex Pelican, great-grandson, and Paul Auerbach, 2nd great-grandson, of Alexander and Rachel Pelican.

Documents

Vital Records

Chaja Blodek/Pelikan, *Indeks urodze 1871-1875*, microfilm 1201163/ Akt 311, LDS Library.

Debora (Pelican) Rosenlicht, death certificate, Kings County, 1931, 20447, New York City Department of Records and Information Services, Municipal Archives, NY, NY. http://w3.ics.uci.edu/dan/cgi-bin/new.cgi

Lea Pelikan, *Akta Zgonów 1869-1870, 1872, 1871, 1873-1875*, microfilm 1895669/Akt 92, LDS Library.

Minnie Pelican, Deaths registered in July-August- September 1897, 1b/290, *England and Wales Civil Registration Indexes,* GRO.

Alexander Pelican-Jane Lazarus, Marriages registered in October-November December 1897, 1c/ 615, *England and Wales Civil Registration Indexes,* GRO.

Census records

Alexander Pelican household, RG12, 284/132, TNA.

Alexander Pelican household, RG13, 269/127, TNA.

Alexander Pelican household, RG14, 1365, TNA.

Alexander Valakan [sic] household, RG11, 451/20, TNA.
Pelikan household, *Spis ludno ci m. Krakowa,* 1870, Polish and Russian, microfilm 2332845, 8-59/p.691, LDS Library.

Other
Email, April 29, 2009, Paul Auerbach to Alex Pelican, referencing A. Palakan.
Hand-written diary, Madeline Rosenlicht Wekselblatt, date unknown, photocopy in possession of Paul Auerbach, Sharon, Massachusetts.
Issuance of Tailor's Licence, Municipal Authority, Head Office, City of Krakow, 30 October 1867, Polish, translated by Barbara Rubinstein and Elizabeth Szeremeta, original in possession of Alex Pelican, Essex, UK.
Letter of Recommendation, Krakau Beth Din, 25 August 1874, Hebrew, translated by Yitzhak Popper et al, original in possession of Alex Pelican, Essex, UK.
Reise-Passe, Reichel Mundel Pelikan, 18 August 1874, German and Polish, translated by Omer Vanvoorden, Wolf-Erich Eckstein, and Andreas J. Schwab, original in possession of Alex Pelican, Essex, UK.
Reise-Passe, Ksiel Pelikan, 4 October 1876, German and Polish, translated by Omer Vanvoorden, Wolf-Erich Eckstein, and Andreas J. Schwab, original in possession of Alex Pelican, Essex, UK.
Tailor's Licence, Ksiel Pelikan, 30 October 1867, Magistrate of Krakow, Polish, translated by Barbara Rubinstein and Elizabeth Szeremeta, original in possession of Alex Pelican, Essex, UK.
Testimonial Regarding Ksiel Pelikan's Apprenticeship with a Master Tailor, 17 July 1860, German, translated by Christel Monsanto, original in possession of Alex Pelican, Essex, UK.
Testimonial Regarding Ksiel Pelikan's Apprenticeship with a Master Tailor, 24 July 1860, Jewish community of Krakow, German, translated by Christel Monsanto and Omer Vanvoorden, original in possession of Alex Pelican, Essex, UK.

Bibliography
Bonar, Andrew A. and Robert Murray McCheyne, *Narrative of a Mission of Inquiry to the Jews from the Church of Scotland in 1839.*http://www.archive.org/ Retrieved 17 February 2011.
'List of London Tailors 1888', Charles Booth Online Archive: Notebooks Relating to the Jewish Community: 55. http://library-2.lse.ac.uk/archives/pdf/Jewish_notebooks.html Retrieved 5 March 2011.
'Cracow – A Riot', *The Jewish Chronicle,* 5 December 1862: 3.
Jones, Revd Harry, *Selections from East and West London,* London: Smith, Elder & Co., 1875. http://www.mernick.org.uk/thhol/eastwest1.htm Retrieved 13 February 2011.
Kershen, Anne J., *Uniting the tailors: trade unionism amongst the tailoring workers of London,* Essex, UK: Routledge, 1995. http://books.google.com/ Retrieved 2 April 2011.
Margoshes, Joseph, *A World Apart. A Memoir of Jewish Life in Nineteenth Century Galicia,* Brighton, MA: Academic Studies Press, 2008. http://books.google.com/Retrieved 17 February 2010.
McCheyne, Robert Murray, *The life and Remains, Letters, Lectures, and Poems of the Rev. Robert Murray McCheyne,* New York: Robert Carter and Brothers, 1860. http://books.google.com/Retrieved 3 February 2011.

Potter, Beatrice, 'East London Labour', *The Nineteenth Century, XXIV* (1888): 176-77, in 'From greener to gov'nor, 1888', *A Documentary History of Jewish Immigrants in Britain, 1840–1920*, David Englander, editor and compiler. Leicester, London & New York: Leicester University Press, 1994.

'Rejoicing of the Law', *The Jewish Chronicle*, 7 July 1892:14.

'The Polish Jew at Home, 1884', 'Report of the Lancet Special Sanitary Commission on the Polish Colony of Jew Tailors', *The Lancet,* 3 May 1884: 817-819, *A Documentary History of Jewish Immigrants in Britain, 1840–1920*, David Englander, editor and compiler, Leicester, London & New York: Leicester University Press, 1994.

Silbershlag, Eisig, *From Renaissance to Renaissance: Hebrew Literature from 1492–1970*, Jersey City, NJ: Ktav Pub. House, 1973.

Sims, R. George, editor, 'Living London, 1902', The Morning Chronicle: Labour and Poor: 1849–1850, Henry Mayhew, Letter VI, *The Victorian Dictionary*, Lee Jackson, compiler. http://www.victorianlondon.org/Retrieved 8 March 2011.

'The New Blood Calumny', *The Voice of Jacob,* 7 June 1844: 163.

'The Tailors' Strike', *The Jewish Chronicle*, 4 October 1889:7.

'Three Times Married', *Lloyd's Weekly Newspaper*, 16 October 1898: 2.

Chapter 7

Mosiek Hauzer

Brzeziny, Congress Poland to Cardiff, Wales, 1889

'He's not a Welshman, he's a Jew.'
Michael Wallach, *How Greeners Came to the Valley.*

Mosiek (Moshe) Hauzer was born in Brzeziny, a market town near Lodz, Poland, where Jewish traders and craftsmen settled in the mid-1500s. Though Jews of this area suffered traditional religious anti-Semitism, they initially enjoyed autonomy and toleration. Conditions in Poland deteriorated sharply in the seventeenth century.

In 1648, Bohdan Chmielnicki, a leader of the Ukrainian Cossacks, branded one of the most evil despots in Jewish history, accused the community of economic exploitation.

His forces, augmented by peasants, tradesmen and nobility, swept through hundreds of towns, destroying synagogues, desecrating *Torahs* and murdering between 100,000 and 500,000 Jews in appalling, unnatural ways. Some were violated or drowned. Some were hacked to pieces or trampled to death by horses. Others were skinned alive, buried alive or sliced into pieces like fish.

Swedish troops, who joined the Cossack rebellion, plundered Brzeziny in 1656. The local priest celebrated their defeat, which was credited to the 'Black Madonna of Czestochowa', by calling for the death of unbelievers, both Swedes and Jews. Townsfolk, fortified by Polish troops, obliged. They massacred forty families, nearly the entire Brzeziny Jewish community.

In the Second Polish Partition in 1795, the Jews of Brzeziny were restricted to marginal occupations, as innkeepers, shopkeepers, distillers, millers and tax collectors.

When Brzeziny was incorporated into Russian-ruled Congress Poland in 1815, however, these restrictions eased. Local Jews became wine dealers, butchers, wagon drivers, harness makers, cotton manufacturers, candlemakers, glaziers and leather, wood, wool and salt merchants. Some worked in the local lumber and textile industries. By 1824 the town supported nearly two hundred tailors, many from the surrounding areas, who specialized in menswear. Jewish Brzeziny also supported a number of bakers. Some like the Hauzers, had been 'in bread', processing, milling and distributing grain, for generations.

The Hauzers probably dealt not only in wheat, but also in hardy rye, which withstands the cold Eastern European climate. In addition to providing fodder, this grain was used to brew beer and distil whisky.

Coarsely ground and leavened with sourdough starter, it also created heavy, satisfying loaves of black bread. An ample slice, washed down with tea or soup, made a hearty breakfast. While most baking was done at home, housewives often baked extra-large loaves in local bakers' ovens, like the Hauzers'.

The Poles who, over the centuries, had suffered a litany of floods, famine, fires, disease, wars, and political unrest, have traditionally considered bread the staff of life, a symbol of good fortune. To this day, many greet guests with loaves and salt and kiss pieces that fall to the ground. Similarly, observant Jews around the world traditionally bless bread at the start of each meal.

Until 1826, when Jews in this region were ordered to adopt surnames, most used traditional son-of patronymics, like David [son-of] Yosef and Yosef [son-of] David. The surname Hauzer, however, appears in Brzeziny records at least a decade earlier. Since Hauzer was a variant of 'hawker' in German, it may have been an occupational nickname.

Perhaps Lewek Hauzer, born in the 1760s, hawked loaves of bread or round poppy-seeded pletzels, from house to house. Perhaps his sons, Abram, Izrael, and Eliasz, hawked their wares as well. However, Mosiek's father, Eliasz Mordka, neither baked nor milled. He bought and sold grain.

Although Brzeziner Jews spent most of the week eking out a living, on Friday afternoons, with the approach of *Shabbes*, they put their earthly cares aside.

Synagogue sextons

used to go through the town and call out, 'Likht tsindn, likht tsindn!' (Candle lighting time!) Right after that you heard their second call, 'Yidn, in shul arayn!' (Jews, into the synagogue!), and at once the Hasidim of the town appeared in the streets in their Shabbosdike (fit for Sabbath) outfit, in a satin zupica (caftan). Some also wore *shtraymekh* (caps edged with fur). The beards and peos (long side curls) were still wet from the mikve (ritual bath). As if with a magic wand all the shops were closed. And you saw clearly how the Sabbath Queen descended over our town. The Hasidic shtiblekh (small Hasidic houses of prayer) became very crowded, and the ardent prayers of Sabbath eve coming from there could be heard far and wide. In their Shabbos clothing ordinary Jews, non-Hasidim, filled the synagogue and the besmedresh … Hardworking artisans also prayed in the besmedresh – tailors, shoemakers, butchers, water carriers, turners (of lathes), and bread bakers. The besmedresh was fuller in wintertime, because a very hot fire was kept burning. Early Shabbos morning the Shabbos-goy [non-Jew who could work on Shabbos], used to light the two large stoves. At the crack of dawn on Shabbos the Book of Psalms readers already had hot tea, and therefore, in winter, they used to sit there more than in the synagogue.

All Jewish boys in Brzeziny, whether their families followed the Gerer *rebbe* or smaller rabbinical courts, studied Hebrew and prayers in *cheder*. However, since the town supported no *yeshivas*, schools of advanced Jewish scholarship, highly educated men there were rare. Just the same, the Enlightenment, which encouraged integration into European secular society, barely affected the community at all.

Life was good, recalls Abraham Rosenberg, especially the food. 'After the harsh winter's groats, and bread and garlic *borscht,* it was a delight to eat *schav* (sorrel) *borscht* with new potatoes, crumbled farmer's cheese with green onions …'

Townsfolk also gathered mushrooms and small hard pears, which they tucked inside straw mattresses to ripen, in the surrounding forests and meadows. Youngsters filled baskets with cherries, gooseberries, currants, blackberries, blueberries, raspberries and strawberries, eating them out of hand. During the heat of summer, housewives served cold, sweet berry soups.

During the winter, people enjoyed preserved fruit syrups and thick jams. Holiday meals, however, were the best of all. Favourites included sweet and peppered *gefilte* fish, *challah,* chopped liver with onions, roast chicken, herring, calves feet jelly, sweet noodle pudding, sweet liquor with ginger cake and compote – all washed down with steaming glasses of tea.

Brzeziny's weekly market, which dated back to medieval times, offered not only a colourful display of local wares, but also welcome diversion from workaday cares. The marketplace was

stuffed with everything good … they sold cotton burkas (hooded cloaks), jackets, trousers, colorful vests, caps with leather visors, fur hats, boots, gaiters, women's shoes, slippers, … shoes with wooden soles … men's underwear, women's bloomers, colorful slips, blouses, aprons, colored ribbons for braids, combs, beads, tin or brass finger rings, bracelets, and cheap watches … all kinds of nosheray (snacks) – caramels, candies, sweet and sour candies, and halvah. The ginger cake baker sold sweet baked goods – honey-ginger cakes, cheesecakes, pastries filled with berries or cherries, long strudels … there also were jugglers, organ grinders with parrots …

Around this time, Brzeziny's Jewish tailors expanded their menswear line to include trousers, vests, jackets and suits. These were produced in innovative, cooperative workshops that featured specialized, economical divisions of labour similar to those in mechanized Britain.

Their low prices, coupled with the town's proximity to a rail service, brought trade from distant corners of the Russian Empire. Brzeziny became one of the largest clothing centre industries in the Russian Empire.

From Bessarabia and Wolyn, from Lithuania and Ukraine descended traveling salesmen, brokers, agents on commission, and bookkeepers … All of Brzeziny became one immense workplace. … The working conditions of that time were dreadful. From three in the morning until late in the evening. Thursday, Jews sewed, cut, and pressed all night long. The need for working hands was great, the wages, good. Even Jews who boasted that they did not have any craftsmen in their family were not able to resist the temptation. Nine to ten-year-old youths were taken out of the khedorim (elementary schools) and sent to 'ler' (apprenticeship) … The entire commerce revolved around tailoring. Shops of accessories, linings, and yarn sprouted up … The town grew.

In 1878, when Mosiek reached the customary age for marriage, he wed Sarah Rywka Goldberg in a religious ceremony. Although his bride hailed from the nearby Piontka district, the newlyweds set up their household in Brzeziny. Hauzer bakeries, mills and grain business could readily support a growing family. Their firstborn, Josef Chaim, arrived three years later.

As more and more people acquired the right to vote, anti-Semitic political parties sprang up across Europe. To attract followers, their podiums rang not only with age-old accusations of deicide and economic exploitation, but also with newer allegations of racial inferiority and international conspiracy.

In 1881, after the assassination of Tsar Alexander II, for which the Jews were blamed, over 200 anti-Jewish riots, called pogroms, erupted in cities and towns across Imperial Russia (today the Ukraine and Poland). They continued for the next three years. *The New York Times* describes a pogrom that swept Kiev in 1881.

> The first procedure of the mob had been to storm the dram shops, and, staving in the brandy casks, to wallow in the spirit. During the period of licence that followed four Jews were killed, 25 women and girls were violated, of whom five died in consequence ... Besides appealing to the blind passions of the mob, the Jew-haters of Russia have ... resorted to more systematic efforts to harass the hapless Israelites ...

They deliberately set Jewish communities ablaze. Because Eastern European towns, primarily built of wood, were heated by fire and illuminated by candlelight, this was easy. Even the smallest spark could set off a conflagration.

> The peasants have a technical name for [their] deliberate firing of towns – the 'red cock' is said to crow ... By the end of June [1881] the 'red cock' had crowed over 15 towns in Western Russia, including Mohilew, containing 25,000 inhabitants; Witebsk with 23,000, and Slonim, with 20,000, as well as smaller towns ... Many thousands of Jews were rendered homeless ...
>
> Every week added to the number of fires in towns inhabited by Jews till [sic], by the end of September, the list extended to 41 towns. To the mass of homeless and penniless creatures in Southern Russia must be added the many victims of pillage ... It is possible that an aggregate of a hundred thousand Jewish families have thus been reduced to poverty.

Although these events surely grieved Brzeziner Jews, they occurred many days' journey away.

Several months later, however, Russian-incited anti-Semitism struck closer to home. In nearby Warsaw, writes historian S. M. Dubnow,

> On the Catholic Christmas Day, when the Church of the Holy Cross was crowded with worshippers, somebody suddenly shouted, 'Fire!' ... in the terrible panic that ensued twenty-nine persons were crushed to death, and many others were maimed. The alarm proved a false one. There was no trace of a fire ... and nobody doubted but the alarm had been given by pick-pockets ... who had resorted to this well

known trick to rob the public during the panic. But right there ... gazing at the bodies of the victims, some unknown person spread the rumor ... that two Jewish pick-pockets had been caught in the church. At that moment whistles were suddenly heard ... The street mob began to assault the Jews who happened to pass by, and started ... to attack the Jewish stores, saloons, and residences ... there were but few policemen and soldiers on hand – which circumstance stimulated the rioters in their further activity ... some fifteen hundred Jewish residences, business places, and houses of prayer had been demolished and pillaged, and twenty-four Jews had been wounded ...

Conditions deteriorated further. In 1882 Tsar Alexander III restricted Jewish settlement, limited their legal rights and forbade business transactions on Sundays and Christian holidays. In response to these 'May Laws', as they were called, massive waves of Russian-Jewish refugees began to make their way west.

Life got harder still. Natural fires swept the town both in 1884, when their second son Pinkus was born, and in 1886, leaving tens of families homeless. By the time their daughters, Millie and Chane, arrived two years later, educational quotas had been imposed, certain professions forbidden, occupational licences revoked, and anti-Semitic violence continued unabated. In 1890, mass expulsions from Moscow and Kiev left many Jews homeless and many more anxious about their futures.

In response, millions gathered scant belongings, bid their families farewell, crossed Austro-Hungary or Germany by cheap night trains, then boarded ships in Hamburg, Rotterdam, Bremen, Antwerp, or Amsterdam for distant ports.

Mosiek and his family, part of this great migration, arrived in London in 1889. They settled at Umberston Street in poverty-stricken St George-in-the-East, an area crowded with Polish-Russian craftsmen. Their two-room rented home, probably a narrow, back-to-back terrace, was described as a 'provision shop', and Mosiek a 'provision dealer', or grocer. Dealing from a front-room shop put him a rung above barrow boys or costermongers, who hawked their wares from wheel barrows or manned stalls at outdoor markets. But space was tight, especially when Marks, their fourth child, arrived within the year.

A certain Mrs Brewer, like many of the English, found newcomers, such as the Hauzers, exceedingly strange.

... I must be in some far-off country ... The names over the shops were foreign, the wares were advertised in an unknown tongue ... the people in the streets were not of our type, and when I addressed them in English the majority of them shook their heads. … to have reached their hearts and brains I must have a knowledge of Yiddish … It is difficult to make ones way. Its shops are crowded, barrows with their wares of every kind fill the road … Living and working as they do in one room, they avoid cooking in it as much as possible; their mid-day meal is often very small. It is generally a little fried fish or a cup of weak tea and bread. … I took my stand also in the general shop in the neighbourhood … and if you ever have a desire to realize the value of a penny, and that four farthings make a penny, go there and note the purchases and the purchasers – dear little children scarcely able to lisp the language, and those tiny arms when raised cannot reach the counter, coming in rapidly one after another with a halfpenny tightly clasped in the hand as if it were of priceless value, asking for a farthing's worth of tea … a farthing's worth of flour, of milk, of soap …

Members of the Anglo-Jewish community were also dismayed at the scope and impoverishment of their Yiddish-speaking, immigrant brothers. Although their charitable organizations provided brief financial aid, they actively encouraged these newcomers to move on – to America, Canada, anywhere.

According to Bermant, oldtimers, through industry and perseverence, had assimilated into real Englishmen. Their sons were entering public schools and universities, and they prospered in trade and live genteel lives

behind the shrubberied walks of Kilburn and the arbours of Hampstead, solid members of a solid middle-class. And now suddenly there came this rude remainder of their rude beginnings. It was no good explaining that the denizens of Whitechapel were one type of Jew and those of Hampstead another. To the Gentile all Jews were alike. There was only one thing the old community could do, and that was to Anglicize the new.

Most immigrants, however, were more concerned with making a living than learning English mores and manners. Since competition was keen, and profits low, Moziek probably laboured long hours in his grocery. Along with perishables, he may have stocked staples like tea, coffee, salt, sugar, jams, herring and a mouth-puckering favourite, pickles.

Pickled cucumbers [observed Edmund Yates in 1879], are never eat[en] by anybody but Jews, and never seen elsewhere; they're said to be

reg'lar good eating, but I never heard tell of a Christian who tried one.
But the Jews – Lor'bless you – they hold 'em in their fists, and bite away
at 'em like boys do at lollipops! … the denizens thereof will eat pickles
at any time, no matter whether onions, cauliflower, cabbage, or what
not, and will drink the pickle-liquor 'as you would a glass of sherry'.

By 1892, Mosiek Hauzer, now known as Morris Hauser, had apparently
had enough of London. Life in the provinces, which offered ample work
opportunities, little discrimination, and fewer urban vices than London,
appealed to new immigrants. Although sizable Jewish communities existed
in Manchester, Leeds and Liverpool, Morris settled his family in Cardiff,
Wales. He was probably enticed by the town's dynamic orthodox Jewish
community, relatively small size, growing prosperity and its large immigrant
population, which may have already welcomed fellow Brzeziners.

Jews evidently first reached Wales in 1749. From the 1870s on, as Britain's
iron and steel industries expanded, they were welcomed in nearly every town
and village of the coal and iron-rich Welsh Valleys.

The Welsh, in fact, had long taken interest in Jews. Some eighteenth-
century Welsh scholars even believed that their countrymen were descended
from Japhet, a son of Noah. Many also believed that the Welsh language,
which had been forbidden in public since 1536, was rooted in Hebrew.

In the mid-nineteenth century, Welsh evangelist Protestants, deeply
influenced by the Old Testament, believed that converting Jews (followed by
their return to the Holy Land), would hasten Christ's Second Coming.
Richard Mills and the Reverend N. Cynhafal Jones found, however, that

> there is no nation under heaven so difficult to draw close to, and to
> bring the light and power of the gospel to bear upon, as the Jewish
> people. It has shut itself up in such seclusion from everyone else; has
> accustomed itself to look down with such distain on the nations, and
> has raised such thick walls of prejudice around itself, that it is almost
> impossible for anyone to get through to it in any way, excepting only
> to do business …

Despite clear differences, the Welsh and the Jews shared rich cultural
histories, as well as a struggle to maintain their identities. So over the years,
they often regarded one other with admiration and affection. Yet in the eyes
of some, Jews would always be outsiders. Once asked about a local resident,
for example, a Welshman answered, 'He's not a Welshman, he's a Jew'.

Early Jewish arrivals to the Welsh Valleys typically eked out their livings as
packmen. Michael Wallach reveals that

in these places [packmen] had plenty of practice in walking across the hills … summer and winter, rain or shine (mostly rain) … an alien figure bent low under his outsize pack … for mile after lonely mile. At the mining village tucked away beneath a dark hill, children greet him with: 'The packman has come!' He knocks on doors, his only English words, 'anything wanting?' (Welsh is a double-sealed book.)

By the time Morris arrived, however, many Jews were exchanging their peddler packs for shops, or purchasing properties to rent out. Morris first opened a general shop in Butetown, a rough working-class neighbourhood outside Cardiff, alongside Jewish watchmakers, jewellers, slop-sellers, tailors and pawnbrokers. In about 1891, the family welcomed another son, Simon.

Then tragedy struck. In 1897, Morris' youngest daughter Annie, 9, died of pneumonia, a complication of measles. Four years later, Sarah Hauser, 40 years old, bore her last child, Esther.

Within weeks of her birth, Morris relocated his family, along with a servant girl, to a spacious four-room house at Bridge Street in central Cardiff. With the help of an assistant, he worked as grocer and tobacconist, both traditional Jewish occupations. Since everyone had to eat and most working men smoked constantly, often sending an ounce of tobacco up in smoke each day, he prospered.

Sarah, whose business acumen was legendary, was his trusted advisor. Yet even in this new world, she retained her Old World ways. For the length of her days, she forbid writing on *Shabbes*, wore a traditional wig and kept her money purse under her overskirt like a Polish peasant. Morris, who also remained observant all his life, was a member of both Cardiff's Cathedral Road Synagogue and its *Hasidic Besmedresh* congregation.

By 1901, Morris was fashioning picture frames, a craft popular with Jewish immigrants, at 23 Bridge Street, running a pawn shop at 25 Bridge Street as well as selling drapery at 31 Bridge Street. His family of seven, plus a servant, shared a four-room home on Bridge Street as well, just a few doors down.

In addition to these trades, Morris also became a 'wardrobe' dealer, selling second-hand clothes. By 1906, when he petitioned for British naturalization, he had also branched into pawnbroking.

Because it requires minimal initial capital, utilizes commercial and interpersonal skills, and offers freedom of self-employment, Jews dominated the South Wales pawnbroking trade. Many were former drapers, used clothing dealers and jewellers.

Licensed pawnbrokers served both the working classes, by offering quick cash for small household items, and the affluent, by advancing loans against more valuable items like watches and jewellery. Some people, however, believed that pawnbrokers callously exploited the poor. Others believed that they dealt in stolen goods or conversely, were allied with the law.

Morris's pawnbroking was so successful that, within the year, the Hauzers moved to a two-storey, single-family terrace house, complete with an attic, at nearby Dispenser Street. By 1911, when Morris had established three more pawnshops, the family moved yet again, to a large home at Clare Street.

Morris and Sarah, now in their fifties, had earned a fair measure of personal and economic security.

Their coal-mining neighbours, who often reacted to hardship with violence, however, had recently suffered lowered wages. To make matters worse, a railway strike, which resulted in a shortage of goods, had raised prices. The economic pressure was evidently too much to bear. Relatively well-off Jews, reputedly renting properties at high prices in Tregedar, some thirty miles from Cardiff, were convenient scapegoats. In August 1911, reports *The Jewish Chronicle*,

Crowds of people were to be seen in the streets [of Tregedar] discussing the railway man's strike … Suddenly a commotion was heard in a bye-street, and there emerged … a band of about 200 young

Morris Hauser, pawnbroker. *Census of England and Wales, 1911* men, singing, shouting, and making hideous noise ... this gang attacked the residence of a Jew ... smashing the windows and greatly terrifying the occupants ... volleys of stones demolished windows ... everything within reach being stolen. ... A rioter rolled up a large bundle of paper ... and was about to set it ablaze and throw it into [a] shop, where there was a large quantity of inflammable goods ... one man was observed carrying his bowler hat half filled with watches. Another was seen carrying away a bedstead on his back, while others played concertinas, accordions, and other musical instruments taken from the wrecked premises ... men and women were rushing along the streets loaded with anything they could carry – clocks, watches, brooches, ornaments, suits of clothes, hats, books, tobacco, cigars, cigarettes, pipes ...

On Monday and Tuesday rioting was general in the mining valleys ... the Riot Act was read and the military were called out, and orders to fix bayonets and clear the streets were found to be necessary ... On all hands there was one cry – that the Jews must be forced out of South Wales.

While some Welsh Jews were quaking, others were apologizing. Maurice Cooperstein, one of Sarah's cousins, for example, blamed the 'uncouth and disputatious nature of the Jewish community for bringing this upon themselves'. Many other Jews across the country, bent on gaining recognition as respectable Englishmen by dissociating themselves with their roots and avoiding attention, agreed.

The Tregedar riots, the most serious in Britain since medieval times, did not shatter relations between the Welsh and the Jews, however. They reflected just economic frustration.

On *Rosh Hashana* in 1914, the Hausers, like many, sent greetings for 'a happy and prosperous New Year' to friends and family nationwide through an advert in *The Jewish Chronicle*. That year they also moved to an even larger three-storey home at Cathedral Road, which Morris had purchased as an investment seventeen years earlier. By then, he also owned Cardiff's Empire Theatre and, along with his sons, a number of other speculative properties.

By 1908, a number of South Welsh Jews were purchasing ships to export mined coal. Morris, in partnership with his sons, bought *Grandest*, a 304-ton, 122-foot long vessel built in Belgium. Within the year, however, while plying the route between London, Swansea, Port Talbot and Rouen, France, the ship became stranded in fog and sank. Though its cargo of anthracite was lost, all eleven crew members survived.

'two photographs by Corn of myself and my husband mounted in gilt frames'. *Miranda Kitchener*

Millie Hauser at parents' graves, Cardiff's Old Cemetery. *Bryan Diamond*

Until 1921, when 'Morris & Sons: pawnbrokers, jewellers, outfitters and ship owners' dissolved their partnership, Morris remained active in business.

When he died in 1923 at age 62, this 'Master Pawnbroker' was buried in Cardiff's Old Cemetery, Highfield Road, mourned by 'his widow and his children, Hyman, Millie, and Esther of Cardiff, Mark of Liverpool, and Samuel of London'. In his will, he left sums to Jewish charities, his estate to his widow, and one hundred pounds to each of his granddaughters 'upon marrying a person of the Jewish religion' (which they did). The remainder was divided among his children.

Sarah, who died eight years later at age 72, lies beside Morris. In addition to bequeathing her household goods, furniture, jewellery and other assets to her children, she willed 'two photographs by Corn [a photographic artist & portrait painter] of myself and my husband mounted in gilt frames' to her son Hyman. Today, these works of art are treasured family heirlooms.

With thanks to Bryan Diamond, great-grandson, and Judith Silver, great-great-niece of Morris and Sarah Hauser.

Documents

Vital records

Annie Hauser, Deaths registered in April-May-June 1897, 11a/177, *England and Wales Civil Registration Indexes*, GRO.

Ela Mordka Chauzer, *Birth, Marriage, and Death Records, 1878–86*, Brzeziny, Polish State Archives, Jewish Records-Indexing-Poland, through www.jewishgen.org

Esther Hauser, Births registered in January-February- March 1901, 11a/383, *England and Wales Civil Registration Indexes*, GRO.

Hana Hauzer, *Records of Births, Marriages, Deaths, 1826–1844*, microfilm 689703/24, LDS Library.

Izrael Hauzer, *Records of Births, Marriages, Deaths, 1845–1856*, microfilm 689704/41, LDS Library.

Marks Hauser, Births registered in July-August-September 1890, 1c/346, *England and Wales Civil Registration Indexes*, GRO.

Morris Hauser, Deaths registered in April-May-June 1923, 11a/405, *England and Wales Civil Registration Indexes*, GRO.

Mortka Hauzer, *Records of Births, Marriages, Deaths, 1826–1844*, microfilm 689703/9, LDS Library.

Mosiek Hauser, *Records of Births, Marriages, Deaths, 1857–1865*, microfilm 689705/48, LDS Library.

Zyskind Hauzer, *Records of Births, Marriages, Deaths, 1826–1844*, microfilm 689703/27, LDS Library.

Census records
Morris Hauser household, RG12, 285/39, TNA.
Morris Hauser household, RG13, 4979/45, TNA.
Morris Hauser household, RG14, 32136/103, TNA.

Other
Mosiek Hauser-Sura Goldberg marriage contract, 5/22, Piatek, Poland, 9 August 1877, Russian, translated by Judith Samson, Polish State Archives, Plock, Poland, photocopy in possession of Bryan Diamond.
Morris Hauser, Naturalization Record, 16288, 13 September 1906, HO 144/832/143604, TNA.
Morris Hauser, handwritten will, K-6, May 1914, original in possession of Bryan Diamond, London UK.
Sara Hauser, will, c/5N, July 1927, District Registrar Llandaff, Wales, photocopy in possession of Bryan Diamond, London, UK.

Bibliography
Bermant, Chaim, *Troubled Eden*, Basic Books, Inc, New York, 1970.
Brewer, Mrs, 'The Jewish Colony in London', *The Sunday Magazine*, XXI (1892): 16-20, 119–23, in 'Are we in London or Lithuania? 1892', *A Documentary History of Jewish Immigrants in Britain, 1840–1920*, David Englander, editor and compiler. Leicester, London & New York: Leicester University Press, 1994, 70–71.
Berg, Jacob-David, 'Our Book'; Abraham Rosenberg, 'Brzezin's Way of Life'; Joseph Shaibowicz, 'Brzezin in History' and 'Towards a History of the Brzezin Kehilah'; Sh. Pinczewski, 'Brzeziner Rabbis and Hasidim'; Yehiel Erlich, 'The Last Kaddish'; in *Brzeziny Memorial Book*, A. Alperin, N. Summer, F. Bussgang, editors, Yiddish, Renee Miller and Judy Howard, translators, New York: Brzeziner Book Committee, 1961. http://www.jewishgen.org/Yizkor/translations.html Retrieved 5 May 2011.
Cardiff and Suburban Names Directory 1901: 404. http://www.historicaldirectories.org Retrieved 3 June 2012.
Cardiff and Suburban Names Directory 1909: 187, 428, 492, 536 http://www.historical directories.org. Retrieved 3 June 2012.
'Corn, Photographic Portrait and Portrait Painter', *Cardiff and Suburban Commercial Directory*, 1914: 511. http://www.historicaldirectories.org
Deaths-Hauser', *The Jewish Chronicle*, 27 February 1931:2.
Dubnow, S. M., *History of the Jews in Russia and Poland, v*ol. II, III, Philadelphia: The Jewish Publication Society of America, 1918. http://www.gutenberg.org/Retrieved 4 May 2011.
'Greetings', *The Jewish Chronicle – New Year Supplement,* 18 September 1914: xiii.
Henriques, Ursula R. Q., editor, *The Jews of South Wales,* Cardiff: University of Wales Press, 1993.
Diamond, Bryan. 'History of the Family of Morris & Sarah Hauser of Cardiff', personal manuscript.
*Kelly's Directory of Monmouthshire & S Wales, 1895, Part 2:*1079. http://www.historical directories.org/Retrieved 3 June 2012.
*Kelly's Directory of Monmouthshire & S Wales, 1895, Part 2:*1224. http://www.historical directories.org/Retrieved 3 June 2012. Kirshenblatt-Gimblett, Barbara. 'Food and Drink',

The YIVO Encyclopedia of Jews in Eastern Europe. http://www. yivoencyclopedia.org/ Retrieved 5 June 2012.

'Notice', *The London Gazette,* 22 March 1921: 2339.

'Remarkable Outbreak: At Tregedar', *The Jewish Chronicle*, 25 August 1911: 8.

'Russian Jewish Horrors', *The New York Times*, 28 January 1882: page unknown.

'The Life of the Rev. John Mills', Richard Mills and the Rev. N. Cynhafal Jones, *The Chosen People: Wales and the Jews*, Grahame Davies, editor, Bridgend, Wales: Seren, 2002:55.

'To the Editor of the Jewish Chronicle', *The Jewish Chronicle*, 22 September 1911: 25.

Wallach, Michael, *'How Greeners Came to the Valley'*, http://www.jewishgen.org/ Retrieved 30 April 2011.

Yates, Edmund, 'The Business of Pleasure', London: George Routledge and Sons, 1879, pp.176–89, *The Victorian Dictionary,* Lee Jackson, compiler. http://www.victorian london.org/ Retrieved 31 March 2011.

Chapter 8

Gershon Bederov

Gorodok, Russian Empire to London, 1902

'Jews and sport? Not for a Yiddishe boy!'
Elliot Tucker, filmmaker.

Gershon Bederov was born in Godorok, some thirty miles north of Russian-ruled Vitebsk, in 1894. Although the town lay amid fertile fields, most of its Jews, half its population, worked in trade or light industry.

Some were tailors, cobblers or harness-makers. Others processed and tanned hides, or manufactured carbonated drinks. Many also laboriously cleaned strands of locally-grown flax, which they bundled and shipped to spinning factories in faraway Moscow and St Petersburg. Since the area boasted vast forests, some hardy souls spent the long winters felling trees. After the spring thaw, they floated their logs down man-made waterways to the Dvina River, which flowed into Riga, a port on the Baltic Sea. Others hand-turned or joined pieces of wood, creating furniture and dinnerware for the local market. During Gorodok's bi-annual fairs, before the summer harvest and in mid-winter, the town buzzed with commerce.

Gorodok's synagogues overflowed with worshippers not only on holidays, but on weekdays as well boys attended traditional *cheder*, while some girls, though they would become wives and mothers, studied arithmetic and Yiddish with private tutors.

In 1830, Gershon's grandfather Itsko (Yitzhak) was conscripted into the Russian Imperial Army. Jewish conscription served a double purpose. It not only supplied the Empire's forces with non-combatant mechanics, administrators, military musicians, cavalry veterinarians and medical personnel but, by requiring its minorities to speak Russian and conform to Russian mores, it also promoted nationalism and assimilation.

Among Eastern European Jews, who traditionally bore no arms, conscription was a terrible tragedy. Many of their sons, thrust or abducted from the spiritual world of *Torah* into a military life with no provision for *kosher* food or, indeed, any Jewish observance at all, forsook Judaism entirely. A few, starving and persecuted, resisted or escaped. Many more, stationed across the vast Russian Empire, were never seen again.

So parents often hid their sons, smuggled them out of the country, dressed them as girls, hired peasants to take their place, or bribed officials to falsify birth certificates. Since the maimed were exempt from the Jewish quota, many Jewish mothers had 'surgeons' break their sons' arms or legs, cut off their fingers or even remove one of their eyes.

Nothing, however, spared 13-year-old Itsko his fate. He, together with boys as young as 5, spent years in a pre-army Cantonist school far from home, studying geometry, geography, numbers, Russian grammar, Russian history, and other subjects required for military service. All cantonists were pressured to convert to Orthodox Christianity. So any who spoke Yiddish, prayed, answered to their Jewish names, or especially, refused baptism, endured beatings, birchings and other tortures. Many died. Since no *kosher* food was available, others starved to death.

On his first leave home, 19-year-old Itsko's parents quickly married him to Genya, his never-before-seen betrothed from childhood. For the next twenty-five years, he served Tsar Nicholas I as a medical doctor in a regular army unit. At the completion of his service, this Nicholaevsky Soldat (Nicholas's soldier) was awarded a parcel of land in Gorodok, along with the customary title, 'Landowner'.

After the 1861 emancipation of the serfs and the arrival of the railways, many peasants abandoned their fields for Russia's industrial centres. Overcrowded and disease-ridden, they became centres of social discontent. So large numbers of people began seeking easier lives elsewhere.

Itsko Bederov's military and medical background clearly broadened his horizons. When his son Menashe came of age, he did not send the boy to learn a trade. Instead, he apparently apprenticed him to a chemist. Eventually, Menashe became responsible for healthcare not only in Gorodok, but in all the neighbouring villages as well.

Through the 1880s, the Jews of the Vitebsk Region were spared the persecution suffered by their brothers in Odessa, Kiev and Warsaw. Religious anti-Semitism, however, fanned by accusations of Jewish economic exploitation and international conspiracy, continued to spread. By 1891, relates *The New York Times*, terrorized artisans, soldiers, merchants and professional Jews, those who had been allowed to live in Moscow, fled the city. All told the same tale, the tailor whose customers had left; the butcher whose business had been ruined because of the exodus; the old men, women, and children begging for help to get away from their surroundings, anything being better than these, amid which they live in constant terror. Homes were destroyed, businesses ruined, families separated and those who were left could only protest that they were not criminals, except that they were charged with being Jews. All expressed a willingness and anxiety to begin life anywhere … so long as they could get away from their oppressors.

Within months, Moscow's Jews received that opportunity. Twenty thousand, hand-cuffed like criminals, were expelled.

That same year, the Russian Empire, which was still predominantly agricultural, suffered a drought that resulted in widespread crop failure. In some areas, even potatoes in the ground shrivelled up in the scorching heat. Although conditions in Gorodok itself remain unknown, the August 1891 *The New York Times* reports a grain riot in neighbouring Vitebsk,

caused by the people's protest against the exportation of rye … The peasants attacked the railroad officials, claiming that no more rye should leave Vitebsk, and severely beat the Jewish grain dealers, who are blamed for the whole trouble. The peasantry also plundered the residences of these grain dealers, and finally combined in an attack upon the railroad station.

The drought, which was followed by famine and cholera, left nearly half a million Russians dead. Many who survived fled the area.

Jewish Enlightenment reached Gorodok toward the twentieth century. Its followers, to encourage contact with the secular world, sponsored a tea house, as well as a Russian library. They also shared a stage with travelling troupes who, along with Russian plays, presented some in Yiddish. To circumvent the prohibition of this forbidden tongue, these were billed as German productions.

Although Menashe Bederov may have been among the most enlightened men in town, his sons, Zalman, Mendel, and Gershon, probably began their studies in *cheder*. At some point, however, the older two may have attended 'The Jewish', a new primary school that offered secular subjects taught in Russian. Gershon was probably too young to attend. He was barely 8 years old when he left Gorodok for good.

His family, Menashe and Malka (Zaboshinska), along with five of six siblings, reached the Vitebsk railway station, their window to the world, by horse-and-cart.

From there, they probably boarded a train either to Riga, some three hundred miles away, or to Libau, farther still. Although both these Baltic port cities lay conveniently within the Russian Empire, their steamers, writes Aubrey Newman,

> were not necessarily luxurious, or even necessarily built for the passenger trade. There are accounts of the use of cattle boats or even timber boats for this purpose, often carrying the normal commercial traffic as well as passengers. The conditions, especially on the cattle boats, are not comfortable reading, especially if one bears in mind that the cattle were the primary concern of their captains and that cattle need constant mucking-out, usually by water pumped over the cattle decks and often percolating over the passengers in the cramped holds below.

Cattle aside, emigrants sailing from Riga or Libau had to plan their journeys carefully. Baltic ports not only freeze over in winter, which shorten their sailing seasons, but entail long voyages around the coasts of Sweden and Denmark. Even passage through Germany's Kiel Canal which, since 1895, connects the Baltic to the North Sea, is quite lengthy.

Instead, millions shortened their journey considerably by travelling overland through Germany. Although passports were not required to enter the country, exit passports were required to depart the Russian Empire. So illegal emigrants often bribed guards to smuggle them over the border or crossed clandestinely through rivers or forests.

Then most made their way by train if they could afford the fare, to Hamburg, a teeming port on the North Sea.

In 1902, George R. Sims, an English journalist, investigating London's slums, 'met' an emigrant steamer that had just arrived from Hamburg.

> The rain is coming down in torrents, and one has to wade through small lakes and rivulets of mud to reach the narrow pathway leading to Irongate Stairs, where the immigrant passengers of the vessel lying at anchor in the Thames are to land. This is a river steamer, and so the wretched immigrants are taken off in small boats and rowed to the steps. Look at them, the men thin and hungry-eyed, the women with their heads bare and only a thin shawl over their shoulders, the children terrified by the swaying of the boat ... What must these people feel as they get their first glimpse of London? All they can see

is a blurred and blotted line of wharves and grim buildings, and when at last they land it is in a dark archway crowded with loafers and touts all busily trying to confuse them, to seize their luggage, almost fighting to get possession of it …

The Bederovs, who arrived in June 1902, must have trod those Irongate Stairs and entered that dark archway along the Thames. But they found London's grim streets festooned with bright buntings and Union Jacks, with merrymakers sporting red, white and blue stripes wound round tall hats and brass bands blaring popular airs in jubilation. That day, Britain was celebrating the end of the Boer War.

The family settled at Christian Street, off Commercial Avenue, in London's desperately overcrowded East End. Here, surrounded by Yiddish-speaking neighbours, ritual baths, Hebrew schools, and *kosher* grocers, bakers, butchers and chicken pluckers, they felt at home. Moreover, if in need, they could turn to an array of small mutual aid societies that, just like in the Old Country, tended the sick, fed the needy and clothed the poor.

Wherever fate takes the Jew, wrote Chaim Bermant, he

has tried to cushion himself against change by taking something of *der heim*, the old country, with him. And the newcomers brought not only their languages, the manners, the clothes, the dishes, of Eastern Europe, they brought their own types of synagogues, the Chevrot (fraternities), like the Plotzker, the Vilner, the Dzikower, the Chevra Shass, the Chevra Mikrah, the Kehal Chassidim, the Chevra Tehilim, and scores of others, small, teeming with life, noisy, crowding each other in the narrow streets and alleys of the East End.

Although the British commonly blamed the congestion of this area on the vast number of Jewish immigrants and their uncommonly high birth rate, there were other causes as well. Because the East End was easily accessible by rail, road and sea, it was becoming increasingly attractive to British manufacturers. So, over time, many homes were replaced by warehouses and industries. Entire streets were razed to make room for expanding breweries. Rents rocketed as housing became more scarce.

People made the best of it, letting and re-letting rooms, and even subletting closets as rooms. 'Give a Jew an inch,' quips Chaim Bermant, 'and he put a bed in it. Give him two, and he took in lodgers.'

As more and more Jews arrived, members of the public, citing their willingness to labour in sweatshop conditions at a time of massive unemployment, accused them of undercutting British labour. Calls for immigration restrictions culminated in the passage of the Aliens Act in 1905. Thereafter, all arrivals were required to show means of support for themselves and their families.

Shortly after arrival, Menashe Bederov anglicized his name to Morris Bedeman. His children, Dvoshka, Rosa, Chava, Zalman, and Chana, became Lea, Rosie, Eva, Solly, and Annie. Gershon, the youngest, became Harry.

Although Morris had been a respected pharmacist in Russia, he never qualified to practise in Britain. Aside from indulging in a bit of private medicine on the side, offering patients brewed white spirits that were 'a cross between vodka and schnapps', he adopted a trade that required no linguistic skills and was always in demand. He became a hairdresser. At some point he also ran a sweet shop and prepared boys for their *Bar Mitzvas*.

Menashe and Malka Bederov, Golden Wedding celebration. *Michael Glazer and Alan Cohen*

116

Although Harry, like most East End boys, continued his Hebrew studies outside school hours until age 13, he also enrolled at St Paul's Whitechapel Primary School at Wellclose Square. On his way to and fro, he passed sooty tenements, bustling workshops, scores of clattering horse-and-wagons, and costers hawking wares from barrows and pickled herring from barrels. Bookies also stood about, accosting passersby.

> … after a great [horse] race has been run and the newspaper is out … Boys on bicycles with reams of pink paper in a cloth bag on their back, scorching through the streets, [toss] bundles to little boys waiting for them at street corners. Off rush the little boys shouting at the tops of their voices, doors and factory gates open, men and boys tumble out in their eagerness to read the latest 'speshul' and mark the winner.

Yet this area, rough as it was, also hosted a variety of amusements. Children enjoyed riding horse-drawn merry-go-rounds or dancing to impromptu barrel-organ or hurdy-gurdy shows along its cobblestone streets. Their parents listened too, either peering from their tenement windows or hauling down orange-crate 'chairs' and joining them. On Saturday nights, East Enders frequently packed the local Yiddish theatres, delighting in melodramatic tales of their lost worlds and values.

After St Paul's , Harry attended the Whitechapel Commercial Street state school, a three-storey building that had been erected at the site of Jack the Ripper's first murder.

The Commercial, though run by the state, boasted so many Jewish students that it followed the Hebrew calendar, encouraged prayer and employed Yiddish-speaking teachers. Like the Jews' Free School, it also strove to produce fully-integrated, model British citizens, ones whose hygiene, dress and decency conformed to standard norms. So Commercial's students not only attended poetry readings and concerts at nearby Toynbee Hall, but were also encouraged to participate in character-building sports.

Harry was a keen swimmer. When he was 14, reveals *The Jewish Chronicle*, he represented Commercial Street in the annual swimming competition of the Jewish Athletic Association Schools' Section.

> It was evident to any visitor … that an event was stirring the locality to greater excitement than even the animation caused … by the day being the one before Erev Yom Kippur [the Day of Atonement, the most solemn Day of the Jewish year]. The bathe had a surging crowd of youngsters at every door … It was quite a sight to see the little mites of girls who had seated themselves on the floor of the gallery, with feet

dangling over the edges, waving handkerchiefs, programmes or straw hats to their schoolfellows cutting through the water, accompanying the action with shrill cries of encouragement or delight.

Local youth clubs, like the Jewish Lads' Brigade, the Brady Street Club, and the Victoria Boys' Club, attracted many teens. Many offered music, art and drama classes, as well as dances, debates, lectures, and concerts. Some operated employment bureaus and savings banks, and organized weekend outings and summer camps. In the spirit of British games and sportsmanship, these clubs also organized chess, billiards, draughts and domino matches, fielded athletic teams, and sponsored gymnastics. Boxing, however, was the hands-down favourite.

Fighting over turf and honour had long been a way of life for East End youth, who were known for their boisterousness and lack of discipline. Indeed, observed Henry Mayhew in 1851,

> cowardice in any shape is despised as being degrading and loathsome, indeed the man who would avoid a fight, is scouted by the whole of the court he lives in. Hence it is important for a lad and even a girl to know how to 'work their fists well' – as expert boxing is called among them. If a coster man or woman [street seller] is struck they are obliged to fight. When a quarrel takes place between two boys, a ring is formed, and the men urge them on to have it out, for they hold that it is a wrong thing to stop a battle, as it causes bad blood for life; whereas, if the lads fight it out they shake hands and forget all about it. Everybody practises fighting …

Despite the image of 'greeners' as weak, fighting, in the East End, was Jewish. Everyone knew that the Heavyweight Boxing Champion of England from 1792 to 1795 was the East End's own 'Mendoza the Jew'.

Despite his slight physique, Mendoza's innovative 'scientific style' – defensive ducking, swerving, blocking, and side-stepping his opponents – was keenly observed and imitated. Besides transforming the sport, Mendoza also transformed the image of the defenceless East End Jew into one worthy of respect.

Ever since, Jewish educators had promoted boxing to build bodies and instill British discipline, patriotism and pride. In Harry's day, local halls were filled with youth who, as of old, tried to box their way out of the neighbourhood. Harry was apparently a sparring partner for some of the best-known boxers of his day. He also enjoyed cricket and earned a football trial with the hard-playing Millwall Football Club.

While many newcomers worked as unskilled labourers, others became upholsterers, cobblers, bootmakers, glaziers or furriers. Jewish women often worked beside their husbands, in addition to manning market stalls, running households and accepting lodgers. Their daughters often left school in their mid-teens, to labour in sweatshops, enter domestic service or do piecework. Their sons, encouraged by the Jewish Board of Guardians, often joined apprentice programmes. At 15, Harry apprenticed to the cabinet-making trade.

Master cabinet-makers often produced a limited number of specialized pieces, creating them from start to finish. Less skilful ones, those who did general cabinetry work, often designed, cut, joined, turned, or carved simple chairs, looking-glass frames, or music cabinets. Others exclusively engraved, veneered, polished or inlaid wooden fancy-work like tea-caddies, glove cases, portable desks or cribbage-boards. Yet all called themselves cabinet-makers.

Harry, to broaden his knowledge of cabinetry, probably moved from one small workshop to another, gaining a variety of skills along the way. At first, he may have learned to prepare wood for production and cut pieces according to sketched designs, while hiding their defects and highlighting their aesthetic qualities.

Although a cabinet-maker's apprenticeship lasted six long years, it was a desirable trade. Working in small, Jewish-run shops not only allowed these craftsmen to observe the Sabbath and the holidays, but since more and more cabinetry shops were opening up all around, it also allowed them to dream. One day, by working long and hard, they too might rent a workspace, buy basic tools and a bit of wood, and become their own masters.

Harry established his own business, 1A Albert Workshops, at Great Pearl Street, Spitalfields, East End, in 1915, while England was deep into war with Germany. As he worked, an attractive tailoress from the Warsaw region, Milly (Jarzembski) Aginsky, caught his eye. 'We passed each other on the way to work every morning – one day I plucked up courage and asked her out – and we have been together ever since,' he recalled. By June they had married.

The couple set up house at Newling Street, then at Brick Lane, both in the East End. Harry relocated his cabinetry shop to nearby Hackney, an area bustling with trade-related Jewish upholsterers, turners, chair-carvers and French-polishers. He, like many, may have initially produced small items, hawking them from a barrow on the street, or through middlemen who hawked them by pony and cart.

As he gained expertise, Harry probably fashioned inexpensive items popular with newly-arrived 'greeners', like gypsy tables, chiffoniers, over mantles, or bedroom suites (which included wooden coal scuttles). Because

Harry Bedeman, British Army, c1919. *Michael Glazer and Alan Cohen*

cabinet-makers were paid by the piece, time was money and immigrants could afford only minimum prices, they worked hard and fast. Speed often superseded quality.

Harry's family, like his business, was also expanding. His firstborn, Morris Isaac, arrived in 1916. When the Tsar was overthrown the following year, Russian-Jewish refugees in Britain were given a choice. They could either serve in the British forces or serve their motherland, a British ally.

Harry was not one to watch as the world turned upside down. The following August, he volunteered for a British Royal Engineers unit that provided military and engineering support to forces in France. He was rejected, however, because of his nationality.

Instead, within weeks, along with four thousand others, he embarked on the long journey back to Russia, probably entrusting Milly and the baby to the care of family members. There he joined Alexander Kerensky's Provisional Army.

When Kerensky established the Russian Provincial Government seven months earlier, his exhausted forces had believed that their days of battle were finally over. To their dismay, however, he continued to honour Russia's obligation to its First World War allies.

So during the 1917 October Revolution, when the Bolsheviks promised everyone 'Peace! Land! Bread!', Kerensky's forces deserted in droves. Harry's corps was disbanded within two months of arrival. Yet he did not return to England immediately. Instead, he headed for Gorodok, where Mendel, his eldest brother, still lived.

Although Mendel earned a fair living by organizing funerals for the local Jewish community, he was blessed with a very large family. So, to earn his keep, Harry ferried people to and from Gorodok to Vitebsk's bustling railway station in a droshky, an open, horse-drawn, four-wheeled carriage.

A few months later, when he had accumulated enough money, Harry headed home – south. Despite widespread civil and military unrest, he made his way hundreds of miles to Odessa, a Ukrainian port on the Black Sea. There he boarded a freighter bound for Constantinople (today Istanbul, Turkey).

From Constantinople, Harry sailed to Saloniki, Greece, arriving in 1919. After failing to obtain permission to leave for Britain, he enlisted in the Army Pay Corps, a formation responsible for military finances, where he served for five months. He was then granted free passage back to Constantinople.

This time around, Harry boarded HMS *Partridge* for British Malta. Once there, he stowed away on a naval steamer that he believed was homeward bound. However, when his ship reached Gibraltar, he was discovered in a half-starved state, taken ashore under escort, then sentenced to fourteen days' imprisonment. Afterwards, deemed a Distressed British Seaman, he was deported to England. Harry finally reached home in August 1919. He had been away for nearly two years.

Harry may have had other daring escapades as well. According to family lore, for example, he once supposedly stowed away to Buenos Aires on a forged passport under the name of Thomas Jefferson.

In any case, once home, Harry wasted no time in getting on with his life.

The couple welcomed their second child, Rosalind Minnie, almost nine months later to the day. Harry also resumed cabinetry work at 2 Newling Street.

The couple then moved to Bethnal Green Road, where their sons Alfred Nathan and Martin were born in 1922 and 1925. Harry, whose cabinetry business was prospering, purchased a small café nearby, converted it into a workshop, then hired four workers. All of them, he noted proudly, were British subjects.

When Harry applied for British nationalization in 1927, his references, a former classmate, a business contact, and a long-term employee, vouched for his honesty, industry, reliability, and his loyalty to the British Realm. The Wholesale Timber Merchants and Importers, a company that regularly lent him 'any reasonable amount of credit', also vouched that his business was financially sound. Milly, by virtue of Harry's naturalization, also became naturalized. Thereafter, Harry insisted that everyone around him speak English, he himself, usually slipped into Yiddish, however, when sharing confidentialities.

During this period, Harry, in addition to running his cabinetry shop, also owned a covered timber yard located near his residence. Through the services of local sawyers, he probably supplied neighbouring workshops with planks of fashionable maple, walnut or English oak cut to their specifications, anything from hefty chunks to paper-thin slices of veneer, sixty to the inch.

When he reached his forties, Harry retired from cabinet-making entirely. He and Milly then settled in Leytonstone, a suburban area in East London, where they opened a greengrocer's shop.

After the Second World War, the Bedemans moved to Crespigny Road in suburban Hendon. Although they were 'not overly religious', they joined the orthodox Ashkenazi Edgware United Synagogue, one of several nearby, for its social events. Though well into retirement, the couple also relocated their greengrocer's shop to nearby Willesden. Since that area was not particularly Jewish, their grandchildren recall, they offered more Jamaican than Jewish delicacies.

In 1946, the Bedemans spent six weeks visiting Milly's brothers, who had settled in the United States. Since Milly was never at ease writing English, Harry filled out her documents as well as his own. Milly, he noted, was 'brown haired, grey eyed, and with health "good all around"'. He too was 'in good health mental and physical'.

The Bedeman children evidently inherited some of Harry's derring-do, his love of adventure. Between 1946 and 1947, they all left Britain for Canada or the United States. Within a few years, however, they all returned.

In 1952, Harry and Milly took their last voyage, visiting their son Morris, who had recently emigrated to Sydney, Australia.

The couple, who spent the rest of their lives in Hendon, celebrated their Golden Wedding anniversary in 1965. The Queen sent 'warmest congratulations' on their sixtieth anniversary.

Harry and Milly Bedeman, Golden Wedding portrait, 1965. *Michael Glazer and Alan Cohen*

Although Milly habitually refrained from lighting the gas on the Sabbath, recalls grandson Michael Glazer, if someone suggested a game of cards, she would be there in a flash. Harry, he adds, remained a lifelong sports fan,

'The Queen sends you warm congratulations'. *Michael Glazer and Alan Cohen*

watching football and boxing matches on television. Like many other Jewish men, he also enjoyed betting on horse races.

Harry died in 1976 and Milly five years later. They lie side by side in Bushey Jewish Cemetery, Bushey, Hertfordshire.

With thanks to Michael Glazer, grandson of Harry and Milly Bedeman

Documents

Vital Records

Harry Bedeman-Milly Aginsky, Marriages registered in April-May-June 1915, 1c/521, *England and Wales Civil Registration Indexes,* GRO.

Bedeman, Harry, Deaths registered in July-August-September 1976, 13/0566, *England and Wales Civil Registration Indexes,* GRO.

Bedeman, Milly, Deaths registered in January-February-March 1981, 13/0591, *England and Wales Civil Registration Indexes,* GRO.

Census Records

Morris Bedenam [sic] household, *Census of England and Wales,* 1911, RG14/1508, TNA. Correspondence

'Archive Inquiry', letter from National Historical Archive of Minsk, Belarus to A. M. Glazer, Oxford, 17 May 2007, referencing Itsko Bederov, Russian, translated by recipient, Bloxam, UK.

Email, 17 August 2011, Michael Glazer to the author, referencing overseas Bedeman trips.

'The Queen sends you warm congratulations', letter, 1975, original in possession of Michael Glazer, Bloxham, UK.

Other

Harry Bedeman, Naturalization Application, 13 May 1927, HO 144/7458, TNA.

Bibliography

Bermant, Chaim, *London's East End: Point of Arrival,* New York: MacMillan Publishing Co, Inc., 1975.

Bermant, Chaim, *Troubled Eden,* Basic Books, Inc., New York, 1970.

Booth, Charles, *Labour and Life of the People,* vol. 1, 1889, London. http://www.archive.org/stream/lifelabourofpeop02boot/lifelabourofpeop02boot_djvu.txt Retrieved 5 August 2011.

Booth, Charles, 'Gambling Amongst the Poor', *Life and Labour of the People in London,* 1903, *The Victorian Dictionary,* Lee Jackson, compiler. http://www.victorianlondon.org Retrieved 22 October 2011.

Domnitch, Larry, *The Cantonists: The Jewish Children's Army of the Tsar,* Englewood, NJ: Devora Publishing, 2003.

'Grain Riots in Russia', *The New York Times,* 29 August 1891: page unknown.

Gregory, Eve and Ann Williams. *City Literacies: Learning to Read Across Generations and Cultures,* London and New York: Routledge, 2000.

'London in Wild Joy Over Peace', *The New York Times,* 3 June 1902: page unknown.

Mayhew, Henry, 'Habits and Amusements of Costermongers', *London Labour and the London Poor; 1851, 1861-2, The Victorian Dictionary,* Lee Jackson, compiler. http://www.victorianlondon.org Retrieved 6 August 2011.

Newman, Aubrey, 'Trains and Shelters and Ships'. http://www2.le.ac.uk/centres/stanley-burton-centre/documents/research/lectures/trains%20shelters%20ships.pdf Retrieved 1 September 2011.

'No Mercy For the Jews', *The New York Times,* 25 February 1892: page unknown.

Samuel, Rafael, *East End Underworld: Chapters in the Life of Arthur Harding,* London:

Routledge & Kegan Paul Ltd, 1981. http://books.google.com/Retrieved 5 October 2011.

Shukman, Harold, *War or Revolution: 1917: Russian Jews and Conscription in Britain,* Middlesex: Vallentine Mitchell & Co Ltd, 2006.

Sims, George R., 'Living London, 1902', *The Morning Chronicle*: Labour and Poor, 1849–50; Henry Mayhew-Letter VI, *The Victorian Dictionary*, Lee Jackson, compiler. http://www.victorianlondon.org Retrieved 6 August 2011.

Sorkin, Dr, 'Memories of Gorodok', *Vitebsk,* Tel Aviv: Vitebsk and the Surrounding Area Immigrant Society in Israel, Tel Aviv, 1957, Hebrew, translated by the author.

'Sports and Pastimes', *The Jewish Chronicle*, 9 October 1908: 19.

'Sports and Pastimes', *The Jewish Chronicle*, 11 February 1910: 29.

'The Bedemans', Mike Glazer, private PowerPoint presentation.

Tucker, Elliot. 'Ghetto Warriors'.http://www.elliottucker.comhttp://www.elliott tucker.com/ Retrieved 15 October 2011

Chapter 9

Chaim Nissan Glazer

Lipcan, Bessarabia, Russian Empire to London, 1905

For Pesach, Oy, dear G-d,
May we live to see, eggs and schmaltz
Yonah Gladstein, The Community of Lipkany Memorial Book, translated from the Hebrew..

Chaim Glazer was born in 1884 in Lipcan, Bessarabia (today Lipcani, Moldova). Jewish *Sephardi* merchants, plying the trade route from Constantinople to Poland, first reached Bessarabia, which lies between the Prut and the Dnieper rivers, in the 1400s. By the early 1700s, when the area was under the control of the Ottoman Empire, Jews, mainly traders, distillers, and innkeepers, had settled there permanently. Over the next century, Imperial Russia occupied Bessarabia five times during its war against the Turks and the Austrian Empire.

In 1812 Bessarabia became part of Russia's Pale of Settlement, an area that Tsarina Catherine The Great had created in 1791 to rid the country of Jewish economic competition. Jews confined to the Pale were doubly taxed, forbidden to lease land and restricted to certain occupations. Because they were also forbidden to settle in cities, villages throughout the Pale, which eventually spanned the Baltic and Black Seas, became overwhelmingly Jewish.

From 1818 until 1835 Bessarabia was autonomous, which spared its Jews the harshest anti-Jewish decrees of the Pale. Moreover, during the reign of Nicholas I, Bessarabian Jews were actively encouraged to settle in its cities. Jewish population swelled further as Jews from other parts of the Pale joined them.

Most Lipcan Jews were tradesmen, shoemakers, furriers, hatmakers, tailors, or worked in the local oil or soap factories. Others were agricultural inspectors, millers, or, like Chaim's father, woodworkers. Since each craft organized its own guild and prayed together, the town hosted not only

> two synagogues, [but] a variety of prayer houses: twelve, the number of the Tribes of Israel – to the pride of the Lipkaners – in them prayed homeowners and craftsmen, Hasidim and Misnagdim. And every Jew had his place in his synagogue And each knew the rest of the congregation and their families well. And thus life continued year after year.

Although Russian was the official language of the land, Lipcan's Jews spoke Yiddish among themselves. Even when the Enlightenment made inroads in the overwhelming *hasidic* character of the town, during the 1830s, most people continued sending their sons to *cheder.* Their daughters, if they studied at all, attended normal schools. Lipcan's Jewish women were destined to buy and sell produce alongside their non-Jewish neighbours.

After hawking wine grapes, apples, sugar beets and wheat at Thursday markets, local peasants stocked up on non-agricultural products, like kerosene, salt and sugar, in Jewish-owned shops. Pickled fish, cut into sixths at a *kopika* a piece and eaten out of hand, was a favourite of all.

Though Christians and Jews shared economic concerns, they remained worlds apart. When local noblemen periodically paraded through town in elegant horse-drawn carriages, bestowing smiles in all directions, for example, Lipcan's Jews doffed their caps 'in blessing'.

The Jewish community also took care of its own. By the late 1800s, it supported a hospital, library, hot meal programme, a savings-and-loan fund for young traders and craftsmen, and services for the elderly. Come winter, volunteers even provided firewood to those without means.

Yet Lipcan winters had their charms. A nearby lake, frozen into a sparkling sports arena 'straight and smooth as the palm of your hand', delighted local youthful skaters. So did sledding and whizzing down hills on homemade skis. Besides, when the Prut River froze over, Jews who attended the synagogue on its far bank, rather than cross by boat or cable-pulled raft, simply strolled over the ice.

During spring thaws, however, the Prut overflowed its banks, flooding the closely-packed Jewish quarters, and sweeping away everything in sight,

> boards, planks of woods, uprooted trees, metal cans, barrels ... Because the floods afflicted only the poor who lived on the riverbank, no one constructed a flood drainage system. People sought shelter with distant friends, and any sympathetic Jewish neighbors, where they waited for the waters to recede.

Although the Prut's thick mud took weeks to dry, some recall that it left puddles perfect for sailing paper boats.

During the summer, Lipcan's youngsters played with rag balls or rolled wheeled hoops with wires. People enjoyed drinking carbonated sweet water or eating 'ice-cream', slender shavings from hay-covered blocks of river ice stored in deep, cool cellars. Many enjoyed drifting in small boats on the lake, simply listening to frogs croak and watching flocks of waterfowl. Others fished or wandered its shores.

Their lives changed abruptly in 1881, when the assassination of Tsar Alexander II triggered anti-Semitic pogroms, large-scale waves of destruction, looting, beatings, rape and murder, across Bessarabia and the Ukraine. The following year, Russia's 'May Laws' forced half a million Jews into the Pale of Settlement, forbade property ownership, and enacted economic restrictions. Additional legislation introduced educational quotas and forbid Jews to sell alcohol, a trade which, for many, had been their main source of income.

By 1885, the Pale, home to some five million Jews, had become the largest Jewish community in the world. Most lived in hopeless poverty.

Life in Lipcan was harsh. Because most of its homes and shops were made of wood, fires, for as long as anyone could remember, periodically swept the town. One night, when Chaim was 8 years old, flames suddenly soared on both sides of the street, sending ashes and sparks skyward. Frightened women, barefoot and half naked, sought safety in the nearby woods. Unemployed Christian builders, it was suspected, caused the conflagration to create work for themselves.

In 1895 flames again leapt from roof to roof in the crowded Jewish quarter. Along with causing widespread panic, it destroyed homes, shops, merchandise, clothing, and trade documents valued at over 13,000 roubles. This time, local authorities blamed the fire on the victims themselves, citing either badly constructed ovens or poor chimney maintenance.

In 1899 parts of Bessarabia suffered a terrible famine brought on by drought. Even root vegetables, deep in the earth, burned up in the scorching heat. When the peasantry became desperate from hunger, troops were sent in to quell their rioting. Farmers, left with no seeds for spring planting, couould no longer feed their horses. So they gave them away for a few *kopeks* or simply watched them die. Typhus followed. The following year, *The Jewish Chronicle* published an emergency appeal by the Central Committee of Alliance Israelite, a Paris-based organization that promotes Jewish self-sufficiency around the world.

The profound distress of the Jews in Russia is well known. In a limited region which the law does not permit them to cross, there are nearly five millions who suffer and struggle: the frightful competition which their congestion itself creates causes a lowering of wages beyond anything that imagination can conceive. To this permanent cause of misery has this year been added famine, with its terrible consequences. In Southern Russia principally in Bessarabia, the harvest has failed , and entire districts are suffering from famine. The Christian peasants receive government subsidies: the Jews can only rely on the support of their coreligionists. In thirty towns, there are thousands of families who have not the means to procure bread. ... these unfortunate people ... are destitute of everything, and a prey to the maladies which extreme misery habitually brings in its wake.

Moreover, noted *The Jewish Chronicle*, the working classes

do not possess the means to pay the rent of a miserable room. Many families, whose heads were formerly hawkers (a calling Jews may no longer follow), have removed with their furniture, and taken up their home in one of the Schools belonging to the community... . all these misfortunes tend to increase the current of emigration …

Two of Chaim's brothers, Joseph and Nathan, evidently left Lipcan in 1900, one bound for New York, the other for Argentina. A year later, his other brothers, Leib and Isaac, left too, apparently settling in Norwich, where they found work as tailors.

Back in Lipcan, their father, Reuben David, continued struggling to make ends meet. In addition to working wood, he purchased pelts from trappers, sometimes taking redheaded Chaim along into the deep woods nearby.

Until 1903 the teen also worked as a lumberjack, floating rafts of logs down the Prut River to the sawmills. Then he apprenticed to an uncle, a printer who lived several hundred miles away in Kishinev, the capital of Bessarabia. If he was there on Easter Sunday, the last day of Passover, in April 1903, he survived an event that would change his life forever.

When a Christian Ukrainian boy was found murdered in a nearby village, locals, incited by the anti-Semitic Bessarabian press, accused the Jews of blood libel, use of his blood to prepare Passover *matzos*. Although the community soon exonerated, passions continued to rise.

A month later, *The New York Times* reported that

gangs of stone masons, carpenters, labourers, and others began to break open the Jewish shops on one of the principal streets of

130

Kishineff. … Windows and doors were smashed in and the contents of the shops either appropriated or thrown into the streets and destroyed. … By Sunday night several streets had been wrecked from end to end, about a dozen Jews killed outright, and close on a hundred severely injured. … early Monday morning … Several thousand moujiks [peasants] had tramped into the town and joined the rioters with hayforks or whatever came first to hand. … The total number of Jews and Jewesses killed is now put down between 60 and 70, and the number of seriously injured at 500. … spikes were driven through a woman's head into the floor, and reports of cases of bodily mutilation have been authenticated.

Soon afterward, eyewitness descriptions of the destruction arrived.

They had axes, shovels, and revolvers. Furniture was broken in splinters, pianos were thrown down from the top floors. They robbed the stores and on the goods they poured kerosene and burned them … A large number of children are among the dead and injured. Girls of tender age have been ravished and mutilated in the most brutal manner. Many Jews are missing. Every day dead bodies are found in cellars and side streets. … We are afraid to leave our homes. Stores are closed, and so are the banks. Parents do not know the whereabouts of their children. Brothers are looking for their sisters.

Chaim's brothers, Leib and Isaac, easily convinced him to join them in Britain. Like many others, the 20 year old probably began the 900-mile trek in Brody, Austro-Hungary, then crossed Germany as cheaply as possible, by foot and horse-and-wagon.

His ship, the German steamer *Silvia*, left Hamburg in autumn 1904. Although his journey was short, it was probably unpleasant. His bunk, reached by descending a companionway, was 'tween deck' in the low, dim, stifling, crowded area directly beneath the ship's main deck.

'Let us imagine ourselves on board a Hamburg boat steaming slowly up the Thames in the early hours of the morning,' wrote Charles Booth in 1889.

In the stern of the vessel we see a mixed crowd of men, women, and children, Polish and Russian Jews, some sitting on their baskets, others with bundles tied up in bright coloured kerchiefs. For the most part they are men between 20 and 40 years of age. … They wear uncouth and dirt-bespattered garments, they mutter to each other in a strange

Hyman Glazer with brother Isaac, c1906. *Alan Cohen and Michael Glazer*

tongue. Scattered among them a few women … in peasant frocks with shawls thrown lightly over their heads; and here and there a child, with prematurely set features, bright eyes and agile movements. Stamped on the countenance and bearing of the men is a look of stubborn patience; in their eyes an indescribable expression of hunted, suffering animals, lit up now and again by tenderness for the young wife or little child, or sharpened into a quick and furtive perception of surrounding circumstances. You address them kindly, they gaze on you with silent suspicion; a coarse German sailor pushes his way amongst them with oaths and curses; they simply move apart without a murmur, and judging from their expression, without a resentful feeling; whilst the women pick up their ragged bundles from out of the way of the intruder with an air of deprecating gentleness.

Between 1903 and 1906, great masses fled pogroms that raged across Bessarabia and the Ukraine. Since most immigrants arrived in Britain without funds, skills, or contacts – indeed, with little but the clothes on their backs – previous arrivals often took them under their wing. Grocery shops remained open long hours to provide them with bread, herring and milk. Synagogues remained open through the night, allowing refugees to bed down on their floors. Mutual aid societies, like the Jewish Soup Kitchen, the Boot and Shoe Guild, the Coal and Fuel Society and the Society for the Provision of Sabbath loaves, aided the lame, sick and needy. In addition, many Jewish East Enders, even those hard pressed themselves, welcomed immigrant children into their homes. The Poor Jews' Temporary Shelter offered short-term housing to thousands of adult men, transmigrants and immigrants alike, for up to 14 days. Its sister organization, the Jewish Association for the Protection of Girls, Women and Children, cared for women and children.

The Jewish Board of Guardians, directed by established Anglo-Jews, operated loan funds and arranged apprenticeships to equip young arrivals with trades. Many feared, however, that extending charity would promote sloth instead of encouraging immigrants to fend for themselves. So, instead of helping all the hapless, the Board repatriated some from whence they came.

Anglo-Jews also feared that the arrival of so many uneducated, needy immigrants – with their strange clothes, foods and religion – would fuel anti-Semitism. It did. The press, reflecting typical British aversion to aliens, described recent arrivals as 'dirty, diseased, and destitute'.

Beatrice Potter, who assisted Charles Booth in his survey of London's slums in 1889, added,

Robbed, outraged, in fear of death and physical torture, the chosen people have swarmed across the Russian frontier, bearing with them, not borrowed 'jewels of silver, and jewels of gold, and raiment,' but a capacity for the silent evasion of the law, a faculty for secretive and illicit dealing, and mingled feelings of contempt and fear for the Christians amongst whom they have dwelt and under whose government they have lived for successive generations.

To the horror of established Anglo-Jewry, many attributed these vices to all Jews in Britain.

British trade unions, concerned about heavy unemployment, also viewed the massive Jewish immigration unfavourably. As Charles Booth observed in 1889,

The unfortunate East End worker, struggling to support his family and keep the wolf from the door ... is met and vanquished by the Jew fresh from Poland or Russia, accustomed to a lower standard of life, and above all of food, than would be possible to a native of these islands ... the force of this competition depends on a continual stream of new-comers. ... For a time it tends to reduce wages and so lower the standard of life, but, apart from a constant influx, this is not its permanent effect. In the long run it is a competition of greater industry and greater skill. We may desire to exclude further arrivals of poor refugees; to do so, if practicable, would be very reasonable, and as popular with the Jews themselves those who are here as with our own people.

Opinions like these led to the passage of the 1905 Aliens Act, which restricted the immigration of paupers and criminals. Although it may not have decreased the actual number of immigrants to Britain, its scrutiny, for the first time, defined them by destination, numbers and nationality.

In the meantime, relates Chaim Bermant, two Jewries were developing in the East End.

one reaching back towards Russia and beyond it to the Second Temple, and the other reconciling itself to this world and to England. The former, even after their children had grown to maturity, kept their old world intact and sought to transmit it as received to the next generation. The snow on their boots never melted.

Chaim, used to wide, open spaces, simply could not abide the East End's overcrowding, clatter of horses and wagons, sooty tenements, pervasive odour of decomposing vegetables and cobblestone alleys slippery with slime. Although its streets rang with the chatter of Yiddish, and familiar bearded men and shawled women thronged its marketplaces, he longed for home. He was not alone. Emanuel Litvinoff, recalls that his tenement, in Whitechapel, East End,

> was a village in miniature, a place of ingathered exiles who supplemented their Jewish speech with phrases in Russian, Polish, or Lithuanian. We sang songs of the ghettoes or folk-tunes of the old Russian Empire and ate the traditional dishes of its countryside. The news came to us in Yiddish newspapers and was usually bad: a pogrom here, a tale of ritual murder there, a tyranny somewhere else … People spoke of Warsaw, Kishinev, Kiev, Kharkov, Odessa as if they were neighbouring suburb.

Despite Chaim's misgivings, he stayed in Britain. Over time, the East End's noise, stench and streets bustling with hatters, cigarette makers, cobblers, cabinetmakers and tradesmen, became less strange. So did its markets, gambling dens, music halls, theatres and street entertainment. In the process, Chaim, like many Chaims before him, became Hyman, Hymie for short. At the time, there were so many Hymies in Britain that Gentiles often referred to all Jews as 'Hymies'.

Though Hyman was short and slight, he evidently began work as an under presser, hefting heavy, steaming irons hundreds of times a day Although under pressing was considered the lowliest job in the tailoring trade, it was essential. Pressers ironed out seams after machinists, usually women, stitched garments together. Especially skilful pressers could 'flatter' even sewing disasters into marketable items.

The tailoring trade, however, was seasonal and unsteady, with tiny sweatshops opening and closing at every turn. In 1906, East End's tailors, influenced by local anarchists, joined their more affluent West End counterparts on strike. Their efforts to improve working conditions, however, failed within a few days.

Moreover, the continual arrival of unskilled newcomers kept under pressers' wages, which were dependent on the pressers who sub-contracted them, extremely low. So 'greeners' like Hyman usually did not remain dependent for long. Within a few months, they sold their skills on the open market or found work with neighbouring sweaters under better conditions.

By the time Hyman married Sarah Romanofsky four years later, he had become a master presser, employing others. His bride, a fur machinist who

Hyman and Sarah Glazer, wedding portrait, 1910. *Alan Cohen and Michael Glazer*

had emigrated from Poltava, Ukraine as a child, signed their marriage contract in English. Hyman signed with his mark, not his name. Since both gave an identical address in Spitalfields, perhaps he was boarding with her family when love bloomed.

The young couple initially made their home at Church Street, Shoreditch. To supplement Hyman's income, they opened a grocery shop, likely packing every corner of their small front room with wares. Though they probably kept long hours, however, they could not make ends meet.

Even when Hyman learned to make alterations and gained experience as a ladies' tailor, jobs remained scarce and pay poor. So the Glazers, whenever they could not pay their rent, packed up and sought new quarters under cover of dark.

By January 1911, when their daughter Rosa was born, the Glazers were living at Globe Road, Mile End, near the Thames. There Sarah was diagnosed with cancer of the liver. Rather than cope on their own, the couple moved into two rooms above her parents' shop on nearby Cable Street, named thus for its original span, the length of a ship's cable. Although the shop was listed as a greengrocer's, her parents actually ran a lodging house for immigrants and seamen from the nearby docks.

Sarah may have been the first patient to undergo radium treatments, a primitive form of radiation therapy, at the Cancer Institute at Mount Vernon Hospital, Northwood, London. Although her therapy was successful, she was left with a gaping wound that would never fully heal. She would need regular dressings for the rest of her life.

During 1912 Britain experienced multiple waves of labour unrest, including railway and miner strikes. That May, thousands of Jewish tailors, meeting in the Great Assembly Hall at Mile End Road, also demanded better workshop conditions, hourly wages, nine-hour workdays, and employment of union members. Two days later, they went on strike. After quickly achieving their aims, they held supportive meetings with their Irish dockworker neighbours, who were also on strike. In addition, many Jewish families cared for hundreds of dockworkers' children.

Despite improved working conditions, Hyman still struggled to support his family. At one time, they were so poor that Sarah supplemented their income by selling matches at the kerbside, with little Rosa in tow.

Lily, their second child, was born in 1913, in one of the successive East End flats where they made their homes. Memories of dashing for shelter during a German Zeppelin attack placed them in Hackney in 1916. The following year, Reuben David, named for Hyman's father, was born at Grove Street, across the Thames.

Hyman and family, c1939. *Alan Cohen and Michael Glazer*

There, the family, hard-pressed as usual, took in seamen lodgers. Several persuaded Sarah to see their ship's doctor about her wound. Although it took two years, he managed to calm it with poultices of soothing, fat-rich Nestle's cream laced with pain-relieving morphine.

When Hyman received his draft notice in January 1918, he requested to join the newly-formed Jewish Battalion, a combination of British volunteers, members of the former Zion Mule Corps and Russian Jews. Instead, probably for medical reasons, he was directed to a local unit of the non-combatant Labour Corps, where most newcomers served. Few Britons believed that foreigners could be trusted on the front lines.

From the moment that Hyman was drafted, Sarah, who had made a fuss when he left, worked incessantly for his release. A week before the Armistice, she succeeded. Since he was honourably discharged on medical grounds – his, not hers, he received a sterling silver lapel war badge, along with an official certificate of entitlement. By then, the family was living at Exmouth Street, Stepney Green, an urban area at the eastern edge of the East End.

In 1923 the couple bought a small drapery and haberdashery shop at Devons Road, East End, with a £100 gift from Mulay Mohammed, a lascar whom they had befriended along the way. From then on, their life improved. Twelve-year-old Rosa, who through their nomadic years had attended no fewer than nine schools, was finally attending, in her own words, 'a proper school'. When she won a scholarship to an art college, one of the first in her school to do so, she was kept home to care for her ailing mother. At 14, however, she left her studies to supplement the family income.

In 1935 Hyman and Sarah purchased a house in Osborne Street, Forest Gate, a residential area in the Borough of Newham, near where Rosa, now married, had settled. During this period, Alan Cohen, one of their grandsons, learned to sew by helping his grandfather 'make pockets' in his workshop.

At the start of the Second World War, Sarah and Hyman, for fear of bombing, left London for Peppard Common. They later moved to nearby Reading, where they remained for the rest of their married lives.

When he was 63, Hyman, and Sarah, by proxy, became British citizens. Although he was officially retired, Hyman still did occasional piecework at home.

In her later years, Sarah, who had become an invalid, spent many hours entertaining visitors in her bedroom. Hyman spent most of his time caring for her and tending their garden. When she died of kidney failure in December 1963, Hyman initially remained in Reading. After a failed cataract operation, however, he moved to the Home for the Jewish Blind in Dorking. There he died at age 97. Sarah and Hyman lie side by side in Bushey Cemetery, Hertfordshire.

Hyman, who like his mother was blessed with red hair, left a colourful legacy. His three children, a number of grandchildren, and a great-grandson all carry the same gene.

With thanks to Alan Cohen and Michael Glazer, grandsons of Hyman and Sarah Glazer.

Documents

Vital Records

Hyman Glazer-Sara Cohen, Marriages registered in January-February- March 1910, 1c/673, *England and Wales Civil Registration Indexes*, GRO.

Hyman Glazer, Deaths registered in April-May-June 1981, 17/0029, *England and Wales Civil Registration Indexes*, GRO.

Other

Chaim Glaser, Passenger List, 373-7 I, VIII, microfilm K 1701-K 2008, S 17363- S 17383, 13116-13183, German. Hamburg State Archives, Bestand.

Hyman Glazer, Medal Index Cards, Labour Corps 273876 Private, WO 372/8/31867, TNA.

Hyman Glazer, Naturalization Application, 1 January 1947, HO 405/19525, TNA.

Hyman Glazer, Soldiers' Documents, First World War 'Burnt Documents', WO363, TNA.

Hyman Glazer, Soldiers' Documents from Pension Claims, First World War, WO364/1361, TNA.

Hyman Glazer, War Office and Air Ministry, Service Medal and Award Rolls, First World War, Silver War Badge, WO 329, 3203, 2958-3255, TNA.

Bibliography

Bermant, Chaim, *London's East End: Point of Arrival*, New York: MacMillan Publishing Co. Inc., 1975.

Bermant, Chaim, *Troubled Eden,* New York: Basic Books, Inc., 1970.

Booth, Charles, *Labour and Life of the People,* vol. 1, London: Williams and Norgate, 1889. http://www.archive.org Retrieved 5 August 2011.

Cohen, Alan, *Glazer Family History*, private manuscript.

'Distress in Bessarabia', *The New York Times,* 7 September 1899: page unknown.

Judge, Edward H., editor. *Easter in Kishinev: Anatomy of a Pogrom,* New York & London: New York University Press, 1992.

Litvinoff, Emanuel, *Journey Through a Small Planet*, Middlesex, England: Penquin Books, 1976.

Lipman, V. D., *Social History of the Jews of England 1850-1950*, London: Watts & Co., 1954.

'More Details of Massacre', *The New York Times*, 17 May 1903: page unknown.

'Peasant Revolt in Bessarabia', *The New York Times*, 9 August 1899: page unknown.

Schwarz, Leo W., *The Jewish Caravan,* New York: Farrar & Rinehart, 1935.

Sims, George R., 'In Alien Land', *Off the Track in London*, Norfolk: Jarrold & Sons, 1911. http://www.mernick.org.uk/Retrieved 22 October 2011.

The Community of Lipkany Memorial Book, Tel Aviv: Association of Lipkany Survivors in Israel, Tel Aviv, 1963, Hebrew, translated by the author. Poem translated by David Goldman. [29 Benihu Ramat Gan, Israel 52215]

'The Distress in Russia, Roumania and Galicia', *The Jewish Chronicle*, 8 June 1900:15.

'The "Continental Sunday" in England', *Sketches from the Life in Petticoat Lane*, *Pall Mall Budget*, 18 April 1889, author unknown. http://www.mernick.org.uk/thhol/contsund.html Retrieved 13 February 2011.

'The Jews in Roumania', *The Jewish Chronicle*, 1 June 1900:13.

'The Kishineff Massacre', *The New York Times*, 14 May 1903: page unknown.

White, Jerry. *Rothschild Buildings: Life in an East End Tenement Block 1887-1920*, London, Boston, and Henley: Routledge & Kegan Paul, 1980.

Chapter 10

Feige 'Fella' Mendzigursky

Leipzig, Germany to Manchester, 1939

*'Learn, learn, learn, they can take everything
from you except your brain'.*
Frieda Mendzigursky's last words to daughters as they
joined *Kindertransport* August 1939.

L eipzig, dubbed 'little Paris' for its vibrant culture, architectural splendour, gardens, dance pavilions and restaurants, has, for nearly a millennium, been a hub of Central European commerce. Although a handful of Jews settled there in the mid-1200s, their permanent community was established only in 1710.

Despite their small numbers and restricted economic privileges, Leipzig Jews, together with scores of Polish and Galician brethren, participated fully in the town's famed tri-annual fairs. They were not alone. In 1836, wrote Redwood Fisher, Italians, Greeks, Turks, Wallachians, 'Armenians', Georgians and Persians also purchased British twist, linen yarn and woollens, French silks, shawls, lace and veils, Swiss embroidered goods and printed cottons, and Russian glue, pig bristles and 'cantharidee,' a popular aphrodisiac.

After 1869, when Leipzig's restrictions on Jewish settlement and commercial laws eased, large numbers of Galician and Polish Orthodox Jews settled within the city proper. Meier Feiwel Mendzigursky, born in Konskie, Russian Poland, arrived, with his wife Ettel Leie Hasenlauf and their five children, around 1904. Like most Jewish immigrants, he was deeply religious. In addition to working as a furrier, he also taught *Torah*.

Over time, many of these newcomers, though clinging to age-old traditions, strove to integrate into German society. In addition to serving their country during the First World War, many contributed culturally, economically, and socially to their adopted land. By the 1920s large numbers had become leaders in business and trade. Meier Feiwel, however, remained observant all his life.

Peisech Mendzigursky, like his father Meier, was a deeply religious, Yiddish-speaking furrier. He was also a commercial traveller dealing in non-*kosher* wine and silver cutlery. His wife, Frieda Wiener, who hailed from a rabbinical family in Poloniczna, Poland (today in the Ukraine), ran a strictly orthodox household, made her own *kosher* raisin wine, lit candles on Friday nights, and observed the Sabbath.

Because she had attended a finishing school, however, she was very progressive for her time. She not only insisted that her family speak High German, but also wore trousers and smoked. The couple, who had married in 1924, welcomed three children in quick succession, Feige (nicknamed Fella), Margo and Adolph.

By the early 1930s post-war Germany was experiencing widespread unemployment, harsh inflation and economic instability. Hitler, as he rose to power, blamed the Jews, whose numbers were growing, for all the country's social and economic problems.

Fella Mendzigursky was 8 years old when Hitler became chancellor of Germany in 1933. Although many cities celebrated with torchlight parades, Leipzig remained relatively quiet, but for Nazi flags flying in windows . Yet the youngster must have felt growing tension as nationwide attacks on Jews and public book burnings became commonplace.

The following June, when 6-year-old Adolph fell ill with pneumonia, Fella recalls, her parents

> put his bed into the dining room to keep him separate because he was so ill. He heard a noise in the street and he said, 'What is that noise?' It was quite a fine day and my mother had the window open to get some fresh air, and it was the Nazis marching along and he wanted to look at what the noise was. And I remember my mother taking him to the window and letting him look out and we saw the SS parading, you know how they did with their goose steps. … I don't think we were particularly frightened.

Just before Etti Lea was born in 1935, Nazi Germany introduced the racial Nuremburg Laws, which separated Jews socially, economically, and legally from their 'Aryan' – Germanic master race – neighbours. Non-Jewish friends and acquaintances, even people whom they had known for years, now turned their backs whenever they neared.

When people active in Jewish congregations, born of Jews, having even one Jewish grandparent, or married to Jews were subsequently defined as Jews, many spouses left their partners. When the fully-assimilated, those who neither practised Judaism nor ascribed to its beliefs, were also defined as Jews, some committed suicide rather than bear the shame.

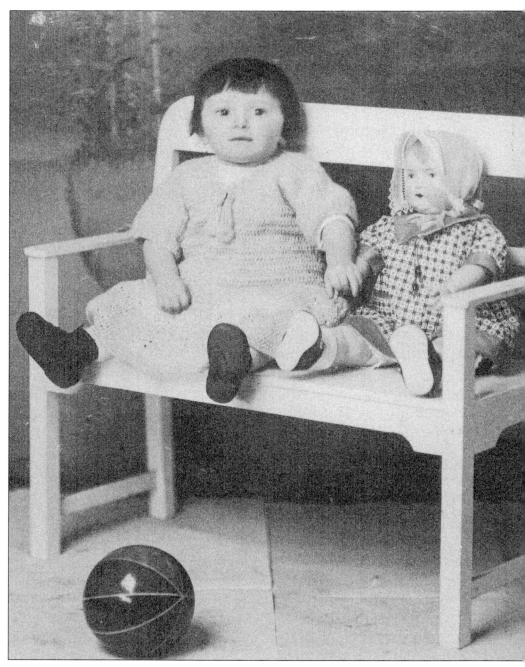

Feige Mendzigursky, c1927. *Judith Elam*

During this period, Fella, like all Jewish children, was barred from attending public school. Instead, she transferred to the Ephraim Carlebach Schule, the only Jewish day school in Leipzig. She came to love it. In addition to studying Jewish subjects, participating in the Zionist-orthodox Mizrachi youth movement and performing gymnastics, a hands-down favourite, she welcomed Carlebach's non-threatening atmosphere. Although some of her non-Jewish teachers wore Nazi Party uniforms to class, they did not openly express anti-Jewish sentiments. Nor did classmates pummel one another with feet and fists.

At first Carlebach's classrooms swelled with new arrivals. As more and more families succeeded in leaving the country, however, attendance dwindled. Jewish professors, recently dismissed from their 'Aryan' posts, replaced those Carlebach teachers who fled to freedom.

A staggering number of anti-Semitic decrees followed. Jews, stripped of their citizenship, could no longer vote, hold public office, eat in restaurants, frequent parks, attend lectures or the theatre, or own bicycles, typewriters, electrical or optical equipment. Many, including Fella's father, were also forbidden to ply their trades.

By 1938 arrests and political detentions in concentration camps had become common. Yet, recalls Fella, 'I don't think we [children] were terribly aware of anything. ... I was then twelve or thirteen. I was much more interested in sports, school, and my friends.'

Germany annexed Austria, with dire repercussions for its Jewish population, in March 1938. The following October, the SS abruptly deported an estimated 12,000 Jews holding Polish passports, even those who had been living in Germany for decades.

Most were left just over the border, near Zbonshn (today Zbaszyn), Poland. Abraham Wiener, Fella's uncle, one of them, later penned

'I was placed on the train
And brought to Zbonshn
Very late, in the middle of the night.
My eyes were teary.
What will we do for the Sabbath?
We receive a fist in our side
Pushed and shoved
Frozen as ice
We only hear moans.'

Because the Poles initially denied these Jews entry, many were stranded without food and shelter in no man's land between the two countries.

145

Herschel Grynszpan, a German-born Polish Jew living in Paris, learning that his parents were among them, in rage, shot a German diplomat to death. In the early hours between 9 and 10 November 1938, German stormtroopers, Hitler Youth and civilians, prompted by the government and armed with crowbars, axes, hammers and incendiary bombs, responded with pogroms across Germany and parts of Austria

In Leipzig, reported American Consul David Buffum,

Three synagogues were fired simultaneously by incendiary bombs and all sacred objects and records desecrated or destroyed, in most cases hurled through the windows and burned in the streets. ... One of the largest clothing stores in the heart of the city was destroyed by flames from incendiary bombs, only the charred walls and gutted roof having been left standing ... It is extremely difficult to believe but the owners of the clothing store were actually charged with setting the fire and on that basis were dragged from their beds at 6 a.m. and clapped into prison. Tactics which closely approached the ghoulish took place at the Jewish cemetery ... tombstones uprooted and graves violated. ... ten corpses were left unburied at this cemetery for a whole week because all gravediggers and cemetery attendants had been arrested.

In Vienna, reported *The New York Times*,

Apartments were raided and searched and gradually some 15,000 arrested Jews were assembled at police stations. ... Many of those arrested were sent to prisons or concentration camps in buses. ... In their panic and misery about fifty Jews, men and women, were reported to have attempted suicide; about twenty succeeded. Scores of bombs were placed in synagogues, blowing out windows and in many cases damaging walls. Floors that had been soaked with kerosene readily caught fire.

In Berlin,

those who participated in anti-Semitic actions had a gay time. ... Older boys unconcernedly threw tables, chairs, and other furniture out of smashed windows. One group moved a piano from a shop into the street and played popular tunes for onlookers. ... The noise of breaking glass and cracking furniture accompanied loud anti-Jewish jeers. When the smashing crew had passed, it looked as if a tornado had swept the street. The pavement was covered with broken glass.

On that night of broken glass, coined *Kristallnacht,* Jewish persecution took a physical, deadly turn as well. Across the country, thousands of Jews were evicted from their homes, orphanages, old age homes and hospitals. More than 30,000 males, aged 16 to 60, were incarcerated in Dachau, Sachsenhausen and Buchenwald concentration camps. In addition, an estimated 35,000 Jews were arrested. Some were beaten to death.

The British government had just refused admission of 10,000 Jewish children to Mandate Palestine. As the scope of Nazi atrocities became clear, however, the British Jewish Refugee Committee approached members of parliament, who precipitated a debate on the deteriorating situation in the House of Commons. The British Cabinet, responding quickly, granted entry to an unspecified number of unaccompanied, predominantly-Jewish children up to the age of 17 on temporary travel visas. Each would require a guarantor posting a fifty pounds sterling bond, to ensure their return to their parents once the danger had past.

British individuals rich and poor, youth groups and schools, Jewish organizations and churches of all denominations initiated a massive fund-raising drive, collecting 500,000 pounds sterling. While doors were fast closing to Jews across Europe, British volunteers were visiting and classifying homes, seeking a suitable solution for each arrival.

Word of the British rescue programme spread quickly through Nazi-occupied Europe. Although scores of desperate parents submitted their children's applications through local Jewish authorities, those who were homeless, threatened with deportation or arrest or whose parents were incarcerated received priority. Those who were accepted had little time to prepare. Parents and guardians, pressing small satchels stuffed with toys and family photos into their hands, bid hasty farewells.

Barely three weeks after *Kristallnacht*, the first *Kindertransport,* a group of children rescued from a Berlin orphanage, reached Britain. Others from Germany soon followed.

Quaker representatives ensured that the children, who had identifying numbers draped about their necks, arrived at centralized departing points safely, then escorted them onward by rail. As their trains passed through German stations lined with portraits of Hitler and draped with Nazi flags, the Gestapo, Germany's secret police, stopped them again and again, rifling through their luggage in search of forbidden items. Once the *kinder* groups arrived safely at the Hook of Holland on the North Sea, the children boarded ferries for Harwich or Southampton port, just a few hours away.

Soon after, transports began arriving from Austria, Czechoslovakia and Poland as well. As related in *Into the Arms of Strangers*, railway stations were crowded with children of all ages, from four to seventeen, and their parents. I think there must have been three hundred … .The children didn't want to leave. The parents said, 'We'll see you in England in a few weeks,' and there was crying and it was bedlam. … The children went with the hope that the parents will follow, or that one day they could come back and they would see them again. [They] did not realize … that only a year-and-a-half later, from the same railway station, trains would go in the other direction to Hitler's slaughterhouses.

In Germany the Jewish round-ups and persecution continued. In Leipzig, the SS dragged elderly Jews to a stream that flows through the zoological park, where, with whips, they forced them into the icy water. Bystanders spit, jeered and pelted them with mud.

Yet only when her father Peisech was taken to a concentration camp, did Fella really begin to grasp the horror that was unfolding.

I will never forget. We had moved to a different flat and over the bathroom was a tiny, little attic. One day we heard the Nazis coming up the stairs … and my father hid in this attic. You couldn't stand upright in it, and he stayed there for about three days and I used to take him food up. … And he came down eventually when we thought the danger had passed, and a few days afterwards they still got him and that's when they sent him to Buchenwald.

Peisech was released six weeks later, beaten black and blue. Like many other inmates, he was ordered to leave the country as soon as possible.

Jews, however, were hampered by recent restrictions on travel abroad. Once they could have taken nearly all their assets with them. Now, even after the forceful transfer of their businesses to 'Aryans', Jewish emigrants were allowed only what they could carry. In addition to arranging German baggage permits, they also had to secure exit papers.

That was not all. Jews also had to obtain entrance visas from their countries of asylum. This was very difficult. The United States and Britain, for example, granted visas only if applicants possessed special skills, arranged sponsors or secured local jobs in advance. Under the circumstances, even professionals like doctors and lawyers were willing to accept menial employment. Through the late 1930s *The Jewish Chronicle* was flooded with desperate requests:

Jewish girl (29) still in Vienna, in great need. Who would help her to get a post?

Married couple: husband, first-class Orthodox cook; wife, all household work; now in Vienna in utmost distress …

Before German concentration camps became extermination camps, securing overseas jobs could also release Jews from incarceration:

German Jew … for years manager of leading shoe house in Germany, speaks English … now in concentration camp, Release him by giving him a job

Typewriter-mechanic (35) mortal danger in Dachau concentration camp, urgently appeals for a job.

For Jews to leave Germany, all their relevant emigration documents, including those from host countries, had to be valid simultaneously. Otherwise, would-be emigrants were obliged to begin the whole process anew. Moreover, most options were prohibitively expensive. Jews fleeing illegally to nearby Poland, The Netherlands, or Belgium had to bribe smugglers. Those bound for Palestine had to purchase British immigration certificates. Many simply could not afford to leave.

'lots of love and kisses' and 'many greetings to your foster parents and many thanks to them'. *Judith Elam*

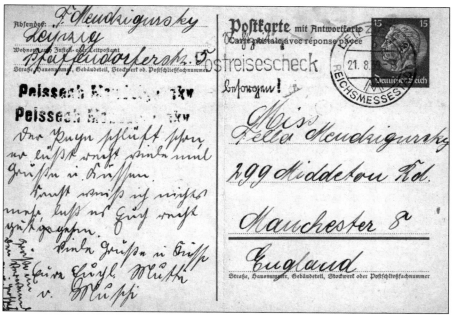

Despite the expense the Mendzigurskys applied immediately for emigration to Britain, where cousins were anxiously awaiting them. Fella, 14, and Margo, 13, who received UK visas through the British Refugee Organization, were able to leave immediately. Peisech, his father Meier, his wife Frieda, and their 3-year-old daughter, Etti Lea, however, stayed behind. Their visas had not yet arrived.

Fella and Margo arrived at Liverpool Street Station, East End, London on 11 August 1939 with the last *kinderstransport* out of Leipzig. Their Bookbinder cousins took them immediately by rail to Manchester. Because they had already taken in five other Mendzigursky refugees, and Peisech was due to arrive shortly, they could not place both girls in the same house. So Fella was placed with friends, the Sulimans, who were also her guarantors. That first night, lonely and frightened, she asked to climb into bed with them.

A few days later, the girls received a postcard desperate for news from Frieda, their mother. She closed with 'lots of love and kisses' and 'many greetings to your foster parents and many thanks to them'.

On 24 August Frieda wrote,

My golden sweet little children, I hope that things are going well. … The good news is that on Wednesday, God willing, Daddy [Peisech] will be leaving here. … My situation will take longer … I hope to be with you soon. Many, many greetings and kisses from your Mummy and Muschi [Etti Lea, their younger sister].

Peisech arrived in Dover, England, on 31 August 1939 aboard the last train out of Germany. Like other refugees expecting to continue on to Shanghai, Palestine, Latin America, and elsewhere, he was granted temporary asylum at Richborough, an abandoned army camp in Sandwich, Kent. There, in 'Kitchener', as the camp was called, he served as acting rabbi. In this capacity, he received the title of 'honorary officer'.

In the meantime Fella was adjusting to a new country, a new home and a new tongue. Like a number of other *kinders,* she was not happy with her new family. As she revealed in *Between Two Worlds,*

I think the reason [these people] gave me a home was they wanted me to help in the house … . They did use me really, to do the housework. And I remember saying to them, 'My mother told me to go to school and learn.'

She never got that chance. After 3 September 1939, when Britain declared war on Nazi Germany, local children were evacuated to the safety of the countryside. Refugees, however, remained in town, with those over the age of 15 sent to work.

Even worse, Fella's grandfather, mother and sister were still stranded in Germany. A British acquaintance remembers that the beautiful Mendzigursky sisters always giggled, but Fella remembers giggling to hide her grief. She was worried sick about her mother. But she was even more upset at leaving little Muschi behind.

When Peisech was released from Kitchener Camp in January 1940, he moved back to Manchester, where he worked as a factory packer, a warehouseman, then a machinist, sewing coats for soldiers. Eventually, Fella, now known as Fay, left her hosts and moved in with Yetta, one of the Bookbinder sisters, where she was very happy. Soon she too, with no former instruction, worked as a machinist sewing gas masks.

Since neither Fay nor Margo had heard from their mother since Britain entered the war, they sent heartbreaking telegrams to Leipzig through the War Organization of the British Red Cross.

They received a response months later, in March 1940. Although Frieda's telegram, sent through the International Red Cross in Geneva, sounded optimistic, her situation, they later learned, was grim. She and Muschi had been relocated to Leipzig's crowded *Juedenhauser*, 'Jew houses' where, for over a year, she had been a factory slave labourer. Yet she had not lost hope. In June, she and Muschi were still applying to leave Germany for Manchester, Raanana, New York … any place offering safe haven.

In July 1940 Peisech was briefly held at the 'hellish' Warth Internment Camp, a disused cotton mill at Bury, Lancashire. From there, along with 14,000 other adult, 'enemy alien' Jewish refugees, he was transferred to the Hutchinson Camp, Douglas, on the Isle of Man, nearly five hours out at sea. Though cut off from the outside world and living under primitive conditions, its inmates, many of whom were highly educated, created a lively cultural and intellectual life, which included lectures, art exhibits, concerts, and even a 'university'. Peisech served as a cantor and acting rabbi.

As the war progressed, Hutchinson Camp internees begged to fight alongside British forces. So when the Pioneer Corps was formed, many volunteered their services. Peisech was rejected, however, for medical reasons.

All this time, he and the girls were anxiously waiting to hear from Frieda and Muschi. Then, in September 1940, the German Blitz against Britain began, initially targeting London. By winter, the Luftwaffe began attacking

Datum: **18.6.40**

Reichsvereinigung der Juden in Deutschland
Be: Abt. Wanderung

Fragebogen.

Name...... Mendzigursky geb.Wiener   Vorname...... Freide Sara   Familienstand...... verh.

Geburtstag...... 3.1.03   Geburtsort...... Toporow/Galiz.   Staatsangehörigkeit...... staatlos

Beruf...... ohne

Jetzige Tätigkeit...... ohne   Mitglied der Jüd Gemeinde...... Ja

Genaue Postanschrift...... Leipzig c 1, Pfaffendorferstr.5,I   Fernruf...... ./.

Sprachkenntnisse...... keine   Fremdenpass Nr.42 M/,gültig bis 20.7.40

Familienangehörige

(Für Angehörige, welche ein gesondertes Auswanderungsvorhaben bearbeiten, ist ein besonderer Fragebogen auszufüllen).

Name	Vorname	Verwandtschafts-grad	Geburtstag und -ort	Beruf	Anschrift, falls nicht wie oben
Mendzigurski	Etti Lea Sara	Tochter	20.12.35 Lpzg.	.-.-	wie oben

Beziehungen im Auslande (Adressen genau angeben)

I. Verwandte:

Name	Vorname	genauer Verwandt-schaftsgrad	Anschrift	seit wann ansässig
Segall	Setta	Kusine	Manchester 8, 34 , Cheetham Hill Rd.	ca. 40 Jahr
Mendzigurski	Chaim Regina	Schwägerin Schwager	Rananah/Pal.	ca. 5 Jahre Kapit.Zert.
Eagle	Fannie	Tante	New York City, 232 East 3rd st.	ca. 40 Jahr

I. Sonstige Beziehungen:

Name	Vorname	Anschrift	seit wann ansässig
		keine	

Frieda Sara Mendzigursky, departure questionnaire, June 1940. *Judith Elam* other cities, Coventry, the industrial cities of the Midlands, the port cities of Liverpool, Southampton and Glasgow, the naval bases of Plymouth and Portsmouth, as well as Belfast in Northern Ireland. But London, with fifty-seven consecutive nights of air raids, suffered most. For nine long months, until the spring of 1941, British civilians found themselves in the front line of the war.

In January 1941 Fay's sister Margo also began working as a machinist. Two months later, though the Blitz raged on, the girls somehow received another telegram from their mother, fraught with worry and begging them to write.

Peisech, in the meantime, was still interned on the Isle of Man. Only in September 1941, fourteen months after his arrival in Britain, did he return to Manchester and his former employer. Yet no further word came from Leipzig. The family later learned that Frieda and Muschi Mendzigursky had been deported to the Riga, Latvia, ghetto on 21 January 1942, one of the coldest days on record.

Herta Rosenthal, who was among the 563 deportees that day, recalls that as they were trucked to the Leipzig railway station, swarms of onlookers, SA and ordinary citizens, jeered, laughing and screaming. When their passenger train stopped in Dresden it took aboard 'a considerable further number of Jews coming from other Saxonian towns', noted A. B. Gottwaldt and D. Schulle. 'The deportees' average age was 42; among them were 56 children up to the age of 10.' Their transport reached Riga three days later. Only forty-seven people survived. The rest, evidently including Frieda and Muschi, had frozen to death.

The following September, hundreds of elderly Jews were deported from Leipzig, Halle, and Weimar to the Theresienstadt Ghetto, supposedly for care in old-age homes. Peisech's father, Meier Feiwel, who was among them, died within months, of typhus.

After the war ended, Peisech worked as a kitchen porter, then a *kosher* kitchen supervisor in Manchester's Springfield and Whittington hospitals. Five years later, he became a British citizen.

Fay, seeking a better-paid machinist job, moved to London in 1947. There, at a Young Austria club for Jewish refugees, she met Max Heinz Nathan. A few months later, they married at the Willesden registry office. Then, at Peisech's insistence, they married again, in a religious ceremony at the Manchester Great Synagogue.

Max, the only child of Werner and Margarete Zerline Nathan, was born in Berlin, Germany. Unlike Fay who was raised in an orthodox home, he was assimilated, well-off, well-dressed and well-educated. His family, including a cousin who had been head of the city's Criminal Police in 1918, and, during

Max Heinz and Fay Nathan – Hindhead, 1950. *Judith Elam*

the Weimar Republic, Vice-President of Berlin's Police Force, was well-connected.

Max's father, ironically descended from illustrious rabbinical lineage, had fought for Germany during the First World War, losing a lung. Before the Second World War, his family had owned a textile business.

At 18, Max was too old to qualify for *Kindertransport*. Fortunately, pipe-laying, a skill that he had acquired in Berlin, proved to be his ticket to Britain in March 1939. He was fortunate to be among the first hundred men selected to refurbish the abandoned 'Kitchener' Camp, where refugees, including Fay's father Peisech, would shortly be interned. For the first four months there, Max did nothing but dig trenches and lay pipes.

Although conditions at Kitchener remained primitive, its 10,000 inmates, an educated lot, not only set up a synagogue and a university, but also established an orchestra, an instrumental quartet, a choir, a dance band and presented weekly standing-room-only shows. Because these men also lent a hand in the nearby fields, they won the hearts of local farmers.

Britain's Anglo-Jews initially feared public hostility at the arrival of these Jewish, German-speaking refugees. Since most were assimilated into Western culture, however, they adjusted easily to British life.

Max joined the Pioneer Corps, dubbed 'The King's Most Loyal Enemy Aliens', in April 1940. His unit, comprised German and Austrian refugees, handled ammunition, built airfields and fortifications, cleared rubble and performed rescues. Then, until April 1944, he served in the newly-formed Royal Electrical and Mechanical Engineers (REME). Afterwards he may have transferred to Britain's elite Intelligence Corps. All told, he devoted four years in defence of his adopted land.

After the war Max located his parents, who had survived the Theresienstadt concentration camp, in the Displaced Persons Camp in Deggendorf, Bavaria. Though they yearned to join him in Great Britain, they eventually settled in a home for survivors in Wurzburg, Bavaria.

The Nathans' eldest daughter, Judith Ellen (named after Etti Lea), was born in 1951. When she was 2 years old, the family visited Max's parents in Germany. After they died, however, Max and Fay swore that they would never set foot there again.

Jacqueline Vera, their second child, arrived in 1954, while Max was working as a life insurance underwriter. Two years later, the family moved into their own home, an indication that they were doing well. Max became a British citizen in 1959, and Fay, as a foreign woman married to a British man, received citizenship as well.

In 1962 Fay's father Peisech died of a stroke. Although he had lost his young son to pneumonia, his father, wife and daughter to the Nazis, and

Max Heinz Nathan, Pioneer Corps. *Judith Elam*

later, his daughter Margo to cancer, he remained kind, humble and deeply religious all his life. He lies in Phillips Park Cemetery, Whitefield.

Over the years, Max Nathan became angry and frustrated with Germany's restitution offers for Jewish Holocaust-era assets because they required the impossible – proof of loss. Finally, in June 1962, he addressed Chancellor Konrad Adenauer directly, in German.

> My father, a Jew, lost his job in 1933. As a result, we were in financial distress, which culminated with Kristallnacht in 1938. To stay alive we sold our furniture at a loss. After the beginning of the war my parents were assigned to a Judenhaus and from there transported to Theresienstadt concentration camp. Their remaining personal effects were confiscated, and their luggage was stolen by the Gestapo in the assembly camp. … your government passed laws that seemed to show … that Germany wanted … to make good on at least the financial damage … But what happened? Using all kinds of pretexts, your officials, some of whom were former Nazis, dragged out the processing of the claims until petitioners and witnesses died … Because the documents of the Gestapo were destroyed by the war there is no damage [?] Everybody knows that the Jew-houses … were sealed! Can the son, who was not there, prove that … the SS who were 'men of honour' stole the luggage? Affidavits? We only take them from Gestapo officials, but not from Jews who survived or are dead …
> I would be glad to receive an answer full of hope, because I am 42 years old and want my claim to be paid out before my 65th birthday.

This was not to be. Six months later, Max died of a heart attack.

At first Fay carried on his insurance business by herself. Later, she became a receptionist at an estate agent's office. Five years after being widowed, she married Julius Shaw, a widower with one daughter. They enjoyed a happy life together. Indeed, after his death in 1984, Fay never considered having even a cup of tea with another man.

Over the years Fay joined various *kindertransport* groups and attended many of their reunions. Though the City of Leipzig repeatedly offered survivors trips 'home', Fay never went. To this day, she wants nothing to do with Germans or Germany.

With thanks to Judith Elam, daughter of Fay Mendzigursky and Max Heinz Nathan

Documents

Vital records

Feige Mendzigursky, birth certificate, 2610/1924, 26 September 1924, German, Leipzig Registry Office, original in possession of Judith Elam, Kihei, Hawaii.

Julius Shaw-Fay Nathan, Marriages registered in April-May-June 1968, 5c/437, *England and Wales Civil Registration Indexes*, GRO.

Max Heinz Nathan, birth certificate, 367, 5 May 1920, German, Charlottenburg-Wilmersdorf Berlin Registry Office, original in possession of Judith Elam, Kihei, Hawaii.

Max Heinz Nathan-Fay Mendzigursky, marriage contract, 9 *Kislev* 5709, Hebrew, English abstract, Manchester Great Synagogue, Salford, Greater Manchester, UK.

Max H. Nathan-Feige Mendzigursky, Marriages registered October-November-December 1948, 5f/484, *England and Wales Civil Registration Indexes*, GRO.

Correspondence

Email, 1 December 2011, Judith Elam to author, referencing Feige Mendzigursky.

Letter, 18 August 1939, Frieda Mendzigursky to Feige and Margo Mendzigursky, German, translated by Wolfgang Fritzsche, original in possession of Judith Elam, Kihei, Hawaii.

Letter, 24 August 1939, Frieda Mendzigursky to Feige and Margo Mendzigursky, German, translator unknown, original in possession of Judith Elam, Kihei,Hawaii.

Postcard, 20 August 1939, Frieda Mendzigursky to Feige and Margo Mendzigursky, German, translated by Wolfgang Fritzsche, original in possession of Judith Elam, Kihei, Hawaii.

Telegram, 23 January 1940, Feige Mendzigursky to Frieda Mendzigursky, original in possession of Judith Elam, Kihei, Hawaii.

Telegram, 27 March 1940, Frieda Mendzigursky to Feige and Margo Mendzigursky, German, translator unknown, original in possession of Judith Elam, Kihei,Hawaii.

Telegram, 7 August 1940, Feige Mendzigursky to Frieda Mendzigursky, Manchester, UK, to Leipzig, Germany, original in possession of Judith Elam, Kihei,Hawaii.

Letter, 30 June 1962, Max Nathan to Konrad Adenauer, German, translator unknown, typewritten carbon copy in possession of Judith Elam, Kihei,Hawaii.

Other

Frieda Sara Mendzigursky, Departure Questionnaire, 18 June 1940,

German, *Reichsvereinigung der Jueden in Deutschland* [National Association of the Jews in Germany], original in possession of Judith Elam, Kihei, Hawaii.

Feige Mendzigurski, *Kindertransport* Record, 8842/9334, 11 August 1939, German, The Association of Jewish Refugees, original in possession of Judith Elam, Kihei, Hawaii.

Feige Fay Nathan, Naturalization Certificate, R3/50087, HO 334/700, TNA.

Feige Mendzigursky, Nationalization Appeal Decision, PRO/HO396/60/443, TNA.

Max Heinz Nathan, Naturalization record, HO 334/429/57131, BNA57131, TNA.

Peisech Mendzigursky, Hutchinson Registration Form, J/A59767, Isle of Man, 9 June 1941, HO Aliens Department, TNA.

Peisech Mendzigursky, Naturalization record, HO 334/353/19079, 25 May 1951, TNA.

Peisech Israel Mendzigursky, Police Report, 15 March 1951, Salford City Police, Box 5, Book 2/ 2224E. carbon copy in possession of Judith Elam, Kihei, Hawaii

Soldier's Service Pay Book, Max Heinz Nathan, April 1940–1944, REME Records Leicester, original in possession of Judith Elam, Kihei, Hawaii.

Bibliography

'All Vienna's Synagogues Attacked; Fires and Bombs Wreck 18 of 21', *The New York Times*, 11 November 1938:1.

Bentwich, Norman, 'The Richborough Camp and the Alien Solders 1939–1945,' *They Found Refuge: An Account of British Jewry's Work for Victims of Nazi Oppression.* London: Cresset Press, 1956, 102-114. http://books.google.com/ Retrieved 10 January 2012.

Buffum, David, 'Crystal Night', *Leipzig, Report on Kristallnacht by American Consul in Leipzig. Nuremberg Document L 202, J. Noakes & J. Pridham Documents on Nazism 1919–1945,* vol. unknown, London: publisher not noted, 1974:473-475. http://www.zupdom.com Retrieved 29 February 2012.

Feldberg, Rachel, *Between Two Worlds*, Otley, West Yorkshire, UK: Random Acts Music Theatre, 2002.

Fisher, Redwood, editor and publisher, *Fisher's National Magazine and Industrial Record,* vol. 3. NY: 1846:210-211. http://www.archive.org Retrieved 5 February 2012.

'From the Testimony of Hillel Shechter about Jewish Life in Leipzig During the 1930's,' Yad VaShem, Shoah Resource Center. http://www1.yadvashem.org Retrieved 10 December 2011.

Gottwaldt, Alfred Bernd and Diana Schulle, *Die Judendeportationen aus Deutschen Reich, 1941–1945: Eine Kommentierte Chronologie.* Wiesbaden: Marixvertag, 2005. German, translator unknown. Retrieved 4 March 2012.

Harris, Mark Jonathan, and Deborah Oppenheimer, *Into the Arms of Strangers*. New York and London: Bloomsbury Publishers, 2000.

Johnson, Eric Arthur and Karl-Heinz Reuband, *What We Knew: Terror, Mass Murder and Everyday Life in Nazi Germany: An Oral History.* New York: Basic Books, 2005.

Mann, Fred, *A Drastic Turn of Destiny.* Toronto, Canada: The Azrieli Foundation and others, 2009. http://www.azrielifoundation.org Retrieved 25 January 2012.

'Bands Rove Cities,' *The New York Times,* 11 November 1938:1-4.

'Refugee Advertisements', *The Jewish Chronicle,* London, England, 4 August 1939: 3.

'Refugee Advertisements', *The Jewish Chronicle,* London, England, 11 August 1939:3.

'Situations Wanted: Commercial', *The Jewish Chronicle,* 16 December 1938:3.

The Song of Zbaszyn, Abraham Wiener, Yiddish, Yeshaya Metal, translator, *The Forward,* 24 June 1939.

Historic Records

http://www.blankgenealogy.com

Conclusion

*'Whoever saves a single Jewish soul, it is as if he has saved
an entire world.'*

Talmud, Tractate Sanhedrin 37a.

The emigrants featured in this study left not only drought, famine, disease, and persecution behind, but also their friends and loved ones. Most, they knew, they would never see again. Despite this, all were determined to forge new lives in their adopted land.

Although Great Britain embraced, opposed, protected, and accepted them – sometimes all at the same time – these Jewish 'greenies' not only adapted but, each in his own way, prospered.

In time, their roots deepened and their families grew. From their roots have come an estimated five thousand descendants, or more. Research continues. And their families, some of whom have spread from Britain to North America, Australia, and Israel, continue to grow.

Ten people, five thousand descendants … Their miracle – the miracle of Jewish continuity – was the confluence of opportune timing, personal resilience and reliance on tradition.

Glossary

Bar Mitzva (Hebrew). Jewish boys' religious coming of age ritual.

Beit Din (Hebrew). Rabbinical court.

Besmedresh (Yiddish). House of study.

Borscht (Yiddish). Beet soup popular throughout Eastern Europe.

Cheder (Hebrew). Traditional boys' religious elementary school.

Chevra (Hebrew) pl. *Chevros, chavrot.* Group, prayer group.

Chuppa (Hebrew). Canopy. Jews traditionally marry under a *chuppa*, a cloth supported by four poles symbolizing the home that the couple will build together. 'Under the *chuppa*' denotes a religious ceremony.

Eretz-Yisroel (Hebrew). The Land of Israel.

Erev (Hebrew). Evening before, leading into, a Jewish holiday.

Eternal lamp. Lamp that hangs above the ark in every synagogue, symbolizing eternal heavenly presence.

Frum (Yiddish). Pious.

Gaon (Hebrew). Genius. Honorific for an honourable sage.

Gefilte fish (Yiddish). Ashkenazi Jewish dish, featuring ground fish, traditionally poached inside fish skin.

Hasidus (Yiddish). Piety. A branch of Orthodox Judaism that, in contrast to traditional *Talmudic* study, promotes joy, spiritualism and religious fervour.

Hasidim (Yiddish). Followers of *Hasidus.*

Hasidic (Yiddish). Relating to *Hasidus.*

Kehal (Yiddish). Community.

Ketuba (Hebrew), pl. *Ketubot.* Jewish marriage contract.

Kinder (German). Children.

Kosher (Yiddish). Referencing food, conforming to traditional Jewish dietary laws.

Matzo (Hebrew), pl. *Matzos.* Unleavened bread eaten during Passover.

Mikrah (Hebrew). Hebrew Scriptures, including the *Torah*, Prophets, and Writings.

Mikve (Hebrew). Ritual bath.

Minyan (Hebrew). Quorum of ten males required for communal prayer.

Mishnah (Hebrew). Redaction of Jewish oral traditions, compiled in 220 CE.

Misnagdim (Yiddish). Orthodox Jews, centred in Lithuania, who opposed early *Hasidus.*

New Christians. Iberian Jewish converts to Christianity, and their descendants, also known as *conversos* or *Marranos.*

Pesach (Hebrew). Passover, commemorating the deliverance of the ancient Israelites from Egyptian slavery into freedom.

Rabbi (Hebrew). Title given religious scholars.

Rabbinate. Office of the *rabbi.*

Rebbe (Yiddish). Rabbi.

Rosh HaShana (Hebrew). The Jewish New Year, which, along with Yom Kippur, form the Days of Awe.

Shabbes, Shabbos (Yiddish). Sabbath.

Shass (Hebrew). Referring to study of the *Mishnah* and *Talmud.*

Shtiebl (Yiddish), pl. *Shtieblich.* Small, informal place used for communal prayer, gatherings.

Talmud (Hebrew). Authoritative collection of Jewish oral tradition that interprets the *Torah.*

Talmud Torah (Hebrew). The study of *Torah.* Boys' religious school.

Tehilim (Hebrew). Psalms.

Torah (Hebrew). The Five Books of Moses.

Yeshiva (Hebrew). Men's highest school of religious study.

Yiddish. High German dialect mixed with Hebrew, Polish, and Slavic vocabulary, written in Hebrew characters, spoken by *Ashkenazi* Jews.

Yiddishkeit. Jewishness, folk culture and practices of Yiddish-speaking Jews.

Yom Kippur (Hebrew). Day of Atonement, the most solemn day of the Jewish year.

Zionism. Support of a Jewish nationalistic home in *Eretz-Yisroel,* the Land of Israel.

.

Master Source List &
General Sources

Master Sources
Akevoth, Dutch Genealogical Society
Yitzhak Rabin World Center of Jewish Studies
The Hebrew University of Jerusalem, Mount Scopus
Jerusalem, Israel 91905
http://dutchjewry.org/

Charlottenburg-Wilmersdorf Berlin Registry Office
Otto-Sur-Allee 100
10585
Berlin, Germany
http://www.berlin.de/ba-charlottenburg-wilmersdorf/org/standesamt/

Church of Jesus Christ of the Latter-Day Saints (LDS)
Locate Family History Centres throughout the UK and around the world
at https://www.familysearch.org/locations

Departmental Archives of Alpes Maritime
Route de Grenoble
B.P 3007 - CEDEX 3
F - 06201 Nice, France
dad@cg06.fr
mailto:dad@cg06.fr
http://www.cg06.fr/fr/decouvrir-les-am/decouverte-du-patrimoine/les-
archives-departementales

General Registry Office (GRO)
Indexes available online, in many UK libraries, county office records, and
family history societies.
http://www.direct.gov.uk/

Greater Manchester Police Museum & Archives
57a Newton Street

Manchester M1 1ET
UK
Police.Museum@gmp.police.uk
http://www.gmpmuseum.com/

Hamburg State Archives
Kattunbleiche 19
22041 Hamburg, Germany
poststelle@staatsarchiv.hamburg.de
http://www.hamburg.de/staatsarchiv

Leipzig Registry Office
Burgplatz 1
04109 Leipzig, Germany
standesamt@leipzig.de
www.leipzig.de/standesamt

London Metropolitan Archives (LMA)
40 Northampton Road
Clerkenwell, London EC1R 0HB
UK
Ask.Ima@cityoflondon.gov.uk

Manchester Great, New, and Central Synagogue
'Stenecourt', Holden Road
Salford M7 4LN
UK
http://www.stenecourt.com/

National Historical Archive of Belarus
ul. Kropotkina, 55, Minsk, 220002, Belarus
ed@archives.gov.by
http://archives.gov.by/eng/

New York City Municipal Archives
31 Chambers Street, Room 103
New York, NY 10007, USA
http://www.nyc.gov/html/records/home.html

Polish State Archives at Plock
9b, Kazimierza Wielkiego Street

09-400 Plock, Poland
http://www.archiwum.plock.com

Sheffield Archives and Local Studies
52 Shoreham Street, Sheffield, S1 4SP, UK
archives@sheffield.gov.uk
https://www.sheffield.gov.uk
https://www.sheffield.gov.uk/libraries/archives-and-local-studies.html

University of Sheffield Western Bank Library
Sheffield S10 2TN
UK
library@sheffield.ac.uk
http://www.shef.ac.uk/library/special/shefnews

The Association of Jewish Refugees
Jubilee House
Merrion Avenue
Stanmore
Middlesex HA7 4RL
UK
enquiries@ajr.org.uk
http://www.ajr.org.uk

The National Archives (TNA)
Kew,
Richmond,
Surrey, TW9 4DU
UK
www.nationalarchives.gov.uk

The Rothschild Archive
New Court, St Swithin's Lane
London EC4P 4DU
UK
http://www.rothschildarchive.org

Tower Hamlets Local History Library & Archives
277 Bancroft Road
London E1 4DQ
UK

localhistory@towerhamlets.gov.uk
www.towerhamlets.gov.uk

General Sources
Genuki
Comprehensive genealogical reference library relevant to Britain and
Ireland
www.genuki.org.uk

Jewish Encyclopedia
published 1901-1906
http://www.jewishencyclopedia.com/

Jewish Virtual Library
Resources on Jewish history and culture
http://www.jewishvirtuallibrary.org/

JewishGen
Numerous worldwide Jewish genealogical resources
www.jewishgen.org

Moving Here
Includes overview of Jewish migration to Britain, 1885–1945
www.movinghere.org.uk

The Jewish Genealogical Society of Great Britain (JGSGB)
33 Seymour Place, London W1H 5AU
UK
enquiries@jgsgb.org.ukwww.jgsgb.org.uk
http://www.jgsgb.org.uk/

YIVO Encyclopedia of Jews of Eastern Europe
http://www.yivoencyclopedia.org/

Index

Places